Finding God
in the Garden

Finding God in the Garden

BACKYARD REFLECTIONS

ON LIFE, LOVE, AND COMPOST

BALFOUR BRICKNER

LITTLE, BROWN AND COMPANY

BOSTON • NEW YORK • LONDON

FIRST EDITION

The author is grateful for permission to include the following
previously copyrighted material:

Excerpt from "Do Not Go Gentle Into That Good Night" by Dylan Thomas,
from *The Poems of Dylan Thomas*. Copyright © 1952 by Dylan Thomas.
Reprinted by permission of New Directions Publishing Corp. and J. M. Dent.

"when god decided to invent" by E. E. Cummings. Copyright 1944, © 1972, 1991
by the Trustees for the E. E. Cummings Trust; excerpt from "somewhere I have never
travelled, gladly beyond" by E. E. Cummings. Copyright 1931, © 1959, 1991
by the Trustees for the E. E. Cummings Trust. Copyright © 1979 by George
James Firmage, from *Complete Poems: 1904–1962* by E. E. Cummings, edited
by George J. Firmage. Used by permission of Liveright Publishing Corporation.

LIBRARY OF CONGRESS CATALOGING-IN-PUBLICATION DATA

BRICKNER, BALFOUR.
    FINDING GOD IN THE GARDEN : BACKYARD REFLECTIONS ON LIFE, LOVE, AND
COMPOST / BY BALFOUR BRICKNER. — 1ST ED.
        P. CM.
    ISBN 0-316-24871-1
    1. SPIRITUAL LIFE — JUDAISM. 2. GARDENING — RELIGIOUS ASPECTS.
3. GARDENS — RELIGIOUS ASPECTS. I. TITLE.
BM723 .B73 2002
29637'2 — DC21

                                                                    2001038385

10 9 8 7 6 5 4 3 2

Q-FF

TEXT DESIGN BY MERYL SUSSMAN LEVAVI/DIGITEXT

PRINTED IN THE UNITED STATES OF AMERICA

For my daughter, Elisa
1956–1973

"If I can remain even an image
A flash or a smile to you —
I have accomplished something."

E. B.

Contents

Acknowledgments

Writing about gardening is as lonely a chore as gardening itself. Yet one can rarely do either without the help of others. Gardeners rely on the experience and wisdom of those who before them labored in the soil, learned from the effort, and passed their knowledge to the next generation. People who write know how indebted they are to those who surround them for the advice, guidance, and inspiration that turn a vague idea into a reality.

I am either one of the luckiest people in the world or a person who, for reasons I cannot comprehend, the Great One decided to save from self-destruct. How else to explain the extraordinary good fortune of having Arnold Dolin as my editor? If I did not know better I would say our meeting and his willingness to work with me was *bashert* — Yiddish for foreordained. His gentle but firm direction guided me at every turn. He even made rewriting almost a joy. He is an exact and exacting craftsman, but his patience with me was unbounded. He is a legend in the world of publishing, and now I know why he richly deserves his splendid reputation. This volume would never have come to birth without his professional oversight and, I hope, his friendly faith in me.

Arnold introduced me to my agent, Sarah Lazin of Sarah Lazin Books. At a time when I needed all the encouragement I could get, Sarah expressed confidence in the project even before it was warranted. Sarah led me to Little, Brown and through that relationship to Deborah Baker, my editor there. Most of Deborah's trenchant and demanding suggestions have found their way into this book. Deborah Baker is a formidable editor and a fine writer. Her skills reflect the depth of her personal resources. Once again, good fortune smiled kindly on me.

For over a decade, Lawrence Kirschbaum, CEO of Time Warner Books, has watched this book pass through its several permutations. From its earliest incarnation he encouraged me, sometimes chided me, frequently berated me, and suffered with me as I journeyed through the "black holes" of self-doubt and despair. I will always treasure Larry's quiet confidence. Larry is a person who enables.

Doris Brickner was among the first who shared her knowledge with me. She helped me learn how to do more than just look at flowers. She helped me understand the deeper meaning of planting a garden. I am indebted to her for that introduction.

My indebtedness to my assistant, Gloria Adell, can only be hinted at in this brief paragraph. She labored patiently through endless bouts of writing and rewriting, and always she did so with a wonderful sense of humor and a boundless willingness to give of herself. Late hours, frantic calls late in an evening or too early in the morning, frenzied demands for misplaced papers, left her unfazed. Gloria is just that: "gloria." I am acutely grateful and most fortunate.

It is my loving companion, Marcia Soltes, who, to use the words of Dylan Thomas, remains "the force that through the green fuse drives the flower." She is the one who, listening to my poorly conceived ideas at the end of a gardening day, encouraged me to write them down. She conceptualized the book long before I did. When self-confidence would desert me, Marcia would rebuild my shattered ego, directing me back to thought and keyboard. Marcia was and remains that force in my life that drives far more than any flower. Marcia is the sum of all the elements that, regardless of the season, make the garden of my life bloom. It is no accident that it was into the earth of our home in Stockbridge, Massachusetts, I sank the shovel, planted the bed, and enjoyed the first boun-teous armful of flowers that became this book. Woods Whole, as she calls it, has always been her spiritual well. It now also nourishes me.

It is a good life. I am constantly aware of the spirit flow-ing through all that happens to me. I am a most blessed man.

BALFOUR BRICKNER
Woods Whole
Stockbridge, Massachusetts
June 2001

*Finding God
in the Garden*

Introduction

G ardening is a lonely hobby. With no people to talk to, those of us who garden do a lot of talking to the plants and flowers — and even to the weeds. We mutter, we mumble, we groan. Occasionally, as when the tree peonies come into full bloom near the end of May, we "ah!" (Everyone does then. The blooms are sometimes eight inches across, and the colors are breathtaking.) Besides digging and pulling, clipping, spraying, staking, raking, and hauling, we get time to think. And that is how this book began to germinate.

Since I have been a Reform rabbi for more than forty-five years, it is hardly surprising that I began to find some spiritual parallels with what was going on in my garden. Gardening is a hobby I began rather late in life. I certainly had no prior experience or, for that matter, interest in plants and flowers or in growing vegetables. I was a Jewish boy born and raised in a midwestern suburban setting, son of a distinguished Reform rabbi, doing all the things kids do. World War II propelled me into the navy. After the war — with college and seminary behind me — a pulpit in Washington, D.C., marriage, and a young family made their predictable demands. Avocational interests that filled what spare time remained were mostly water related, since by then we had built a summer house on the island of Martha's Vineyard, where boating, sailing, fishing, skin diving, and an occasional tennis game were our way of life. Gardening? Aside from dropping some annuals in a flower box at the beginning of the season, the thought never crossed my mind.

So how did I get into gardening? I certainly was not born to it. When I was a child, my mother had a sizable garden behind our suburban home. I still have a mental image of her talking with the gardener, instructing him about planting this or that. I had as much interest in that garden as a fish has in a coal mine. Perhaps in some very subtle way, my paternal grandfather contributed to my eventual drift toward gardening. We lived next to woods, where, when he visited, Grandpa loved taking me on his walks. He seemed to know the name of every tree. He pointed out growing things on the floor of the woods that I would otherwise have stepped on or over. Without my even knowing it, he probably planted in me a love of nature that must have found good soil somewhere deep inside my subconscious. It first manifested itself through a youthful affection for the Canadian bush, where, during my adolescence, I went to camp and fell in love with canoeing. I could not get enough of the woods and the lakes. Perhaps that early, youthful passion subliminally fed my enduring love of nature, the earth, soil, plants, and growing things.

This ardor did not really blossom until decades later. I had left the Vineyard and, with a new wife in a new life, unexpectedly purchased a home on Shelter Island, a small island wedged between the easternmost arms of Long Island. We called the place Second Site. The house desperately needed landscaping, but our budget was far too tight for such a luxury. So I began to garden. As the bromide goes, "It's a dirty job, but someone has to do it." At first, I dug holes for the dozen or so Japanese black pines we planted as a screen. Next, a corner of the land needed to have a bed dug and prepared. Shelter Island, I discovered, is the mother lode of rocks, and I quickly became an expert on the digging and removal of same.

Clearly, holes in the ground and garden beds are not made to remain empty. They cry out to be filled with trees, plants, flowers. But which ones? I did not have a clue. What I thought I knew was that plants grow in sunshine, but I had no idea that a vast number of plants, such as hostas, azaleas, astilbes, columbines, and rhododendrons, do better in shade. Nor did I know that the composition of the soil is important. Some plants demand acidic soil; others prefer a "sweeter" growing condition, one rich in alkaline.

Shelter Island had one excellent nursery, whose owner and on-site manager, Blaze Laspia, possessed a wonderful, wry sense of humor. If you caught him after the spring sales crush, Blaze gave freely of his vast wisdom. I did not know that, when, as a newcomer to the island and a neophyte, I cautiously approached, list in hand. He knew the property. (Word gets around quickly on a small island, and my immediate neighbor was a "hairy legger," their term for one born and raised there. That meant that the locals knew far more about me than I did about any of them. I spent nearly twenty years on Shelter Island, and that imbalance never changed.) Blaze took one look at my list, a quick glance at me, and my first class in Gardening 101 began. An hour later, I turned up the driveway to Second Site, the back of my station wagon bursting with shrubs and plants, each one marked appropriately: "sun," "shade," "tall — rear of bed," "short — front of bed," "plant in lots of peat moss and leaves," "feed with high-nitrogen plant food," and so on.

Matters soon got out of hand. Land clearing, tree cutting to get some light and a view of Gardiners Bay, root and weed pulling — especially bittersweet root and mean, tough bull thorn (aptly named) — led to more beds and more planting, mainly of perennials, most of which really did bloom magnificently. Suddenly, I was trapped — *addicted* is the better word. There is nothing quite so satisfying as seeing a plant that you have in the ground actually bloom or flower. (Shrubs bloom; plants flower — don't ask me why.)

I began to hear my grandfather telling me about the sanctity of the soil, and I began to believe it. I began to see earth and its capacity to produce trees, shrubs, and plants as something critically important. The predictability of nature, our capacity to discern its order and to plan gardens around that order, overwhelmed me with awe and respect. I began to feel that I had an obligation to at least protect, if not enhance, living matter. The more I saw the ecosystem and the environment around me deteriorate because of nothing more than human greed, the more important it became to enhance my couple of acres. I wanted them to be not just beautiful but also an example of what people who cared about the land could accomplish. It didn't turn out that way, but I do believe we made a good start. There is a well-known rabbinic saying: "It is not incumbent on you to finish the task, but neither are you free to desist from beginning it."

Time and circumstance have had their way. Point of View, our family home on Martha's Vineyard where my three children spent their summers from infancy through young adulthood, was sold long ago. I go to the Vineyard only periodically, and then it is primarily to visit the small Jewish cemetery on the island where, after her tragic death in an accident, we buried our daughter, Elisa, in 1973.

Second Site is also in the hands of another. The new owner tells us how much she enjoys the tree peonies and what a fairyland of blooms the place is in the spring. I like that. It helps make all the sweat that went into that garden seem most worthwhile.

I now spend the seasons in a home in the gentle, lovely Berkshire hills of western Massachusetts. There, in the autumn years of my life, I have rediscovered my earlier passion for the land and nature. What started out as a small bed, which I dug one summer afternoon more to amuse myself than to beautify the place, has become in the past four or five years an extensive, cultivated, time- and money-consuming botanical arena. It has overtaken me. My companion, with whom I share Woods Whole and who sees things from a psychological perspective, thinks I have become obsessive-compulsive about the garden. She may be right. I seem to be unable to drive past a nursery, especially in the late fall, when there are plant and shrub bargains galore.

The more time I have spent in my garden, the more I have realized how much it has to teach me, to teach all of us. I began to see that some of my supposedly far-fetched ideas about how we know God and what law and order mean in the cosmos and to our world are validated by what happens in the garden. I saw how the cycles of birth, growth, death, and decay so evident in a garden are meaningfully mirrored in our lives. I began to learn more about reproduction, sexuality, what is truly miraculous (and what is not), dying, death and rebirth, patience, hope, how nature can and does heal. With every turn of the shovel, as the worms wriggled free of my spade, I saw how that microcosm was a perfect reflection of what was going on in the macrocosm millions of light-years away from and above me. I began to realize that if I looked up, I would better understand what was going on when I looked down, and vice versa. In other words, the more I gardened, the more I began to learn about life, about what religion tries to teach and what faith tries to deepen.

Periodically, I would scribble down some of my random thoughts. Those scraps of paper I left on a nail in my work shed at the end of a gardening day soon became a pile on my desk. Eventually, no longer able to ignore the pile, I picked up the notes and read through them. Tossing aside the doggerel, the clichés, the adolescent nonsense, I began to work on the kernel of an idea. What follows is the distillate of that refining process.

God is in the garden, and anyone can find God there. In fact, God is the Master Gardener. God plans, plants, paints with an incredible palette (we call them flowers), grows, harvests, and conserves. This book is my attempt to share with you what I have learned: how my belief that faith comes last and grows out of strict canons of critical thought and careful reasoning is confirmed by the laws of nature.

I know that in this conviction I am something of an anachronism. Most people have lost faith in reason as a way to find faith. Religious rationalism is not popular today. Emotionalism, feel-good faith, and so-called New Age spirituality are the new trends in religion. But in my view, we ought not abandon reason in our approach to one another and to our God. Discovering the lawfulness of the universe, seeing its orderliness, is the one way we really have to strengthen faith.

Observing Nature as it unfolds in a garden makes that crystal clear to anyone who makes the effort to see it. The garden is a microcosm of our much larger world.

Gardening is dirty, sweaty, sometimes heartbreaking work, but when my hedge of 'Bonica' — a classic shrub rose, the first to win All America Rose Selections honors — breaks into its full, fragrant bloom, I begin to understand and feel spiritual pleasure as no theologian or philosopher has ever taught me. In this book, I try to share that pleasure with you. My hope is that these words will help you find your way down some new paths of spiritual confidence. Maybe you, too, will gain some new and satisfying religious and spiritual insights as something in this garden inspires a new vision. Perhaps that will generate in you a "Wow! I hadn't thought of that before" or "I hadn't seen that before. Isn't it awesome?" That is what gardening is all about. That is what spirituality is all about. That is what this book is all about.

CHAPTER I

Eden: The First Garden

Eden is that old-fashioned House
We dwell in every day
Without suspecting our abode
Until we drive away.

How fair on looking back, the Day
We sauntered from the Door —
Unconscious our returning,
But discover it no more.

Emily Dickinson

H ow can one write a book on gardening and God without starting in the most obvious place? Eden is the
first garden described in any Western religious literature, and
if one accepts what is written about it in the Bible, it must
have been an incredible place. But what did it look like?

Where was it? No one knows or could ever have known. The Eden described in the Bible probably never existed. I think of it as being like that mythical village of Brigadoon — a lovely imaginary place, repository of all our yearnings.

But was there ever such a place as Eden? Could there ever have been? We may find a hint of an answer to such questions from the word itself.

Linguistic scholars tell us that while the Hebrew word *eden* means "delight," the word actually derives from the language of a Middle Eastern civilization, the Sumerians, who predated the Hebrews in that part of the world by some fifteen hundred years. We find in their vocabulary the word *edinu*, meaning "steppe" or "plain." So Eden, a diminutive or corruption of *edinu*, might have been a plain or steppe nestled somewhere between the two great life-giving rivers of the Middle East, the Tigris and Euphrates, the possible sources of our garden's water.

By the time the Hebrews appeared on the scene, the phrase "Garden of Eden" came to signify some mythical after-death place for the righteous, and it lost all geographic meaning. It ceased to be a place and became instead an idea, even an ideal.

As a professional religionist, I know how theologians through the ages have used the story of the Garden of Eden either to create or to justify their own religious views. Later in this chapter, I will deal with one of the more powerful (and damaging) of these ideas, but for now it is as a gardener that I approach this tale. From that perspective, I am uplifted spiritually by the story every time I read it. A garden — and surely that first, most perfect garden — fires the imagination. Imagine its beauty. Imagine its serenity. Within our deepest parts, there seems to be a drive to seek and surround ourselves with beauty, whether through art, music, or great literature. And that is precisely what brings us to appreciate a beautifully designed, exquisitely executed garden.

Rare indeed is the person who does not resonate to a garden. I have seen hundreds of people who did not know a petunia from a privy walk through both public and private gardens enthralled by what they saw. They may have had no knowledge of bloom time or sun requirements; they may have been totally ignorant of, and oblivious to, what it takes to make a plant bloom. But none of this is required for the sheer enjoyment of that combination of shape, color, size, and spatial relationships that helps our senses respond to a garden. I have watched the most cynical people melt into silent wonder as they viewed a mature quince or crab apple tree in full spring bloom. A couple of years ago, I planted a young one, *Malus* 'Indian Summer', along our drive, and it has become a spring traffic hazard. Drivers can't seem to take their eyes off it as they approach our house.

What is there about a garden that generates so much pleasurable response from so many? Perhaps we see the garden as a symbol — a place, yes, but more than a place, a space that represents some fulfillment of homogeneity lacking in our too frequently unsatisfying societies. Perhaps it beckons to us with a simple goodness, a lovely innocence to which we would like to return. A line from the song "Woodstock" captures this longing: "We've got to get ourselves back to the garden." Gardening can represent the simple values — integrity, wholeness, purity — but the compelling power for me lies in its challenge to be creative and in the personal satisfaction that the arduous work of a garden brings. Turning bare space into a place of beauty is a form of birthing. It brings into being the potential hidden in the source. Perhaps God experienced such a feeling when looking down on the results of creation. Nurturing a garden into maturity challenges only the self. It threatens no one. The only things one has to "beat" when gardening are weeds. Gardening can be exhausting, but one rarely grows tired of it. No wonder I find it so hard to stay out of the garden — except, of course, in the dead of winter.

I've done my share of digging in virgin ground, jolting shoulder, elbow, and back as shovel clanged on some humongous, defiant, glacially buried rock resisting, as each one does, every effort to be pried loose from its antediluvian resting spot, and I can assure you that all of us seriously addicted to gardening ask that "what was Eden like?" question. Anyone who knows the pain and the reward of turning lifeless compacted dirt into fertile soil — enriching it with bales of peat moss, bags of rotted cow manure, and compost from an oft-turned pile — must wonder how that first garden got put together. Since Genesis gives us only hints of what paradise must have originally looked like, we have to use our imaginations to complete the picture.

In the beginning, it was "unformed and void" (Gen. 1:2), and if the earliest texts are to be believed, the place must have looked like a bog or swamp, much too wet to plant. God took care of that problem not with the addition of ferns or dozens of moisture-loving plants such as aconitum, astilbes, or turtlehead, but with one sweeping command. So simple. One can almost hear the entire firmament echoing with the sound of the Great One's order: "Let the water below the sky . . . be gathered into one area / That the dry land may appear" (Gen. 1:9).

One would expect that divine bellow to establish a proper and perfect place, and in fact, everything seems to have grown just right in Eden: "And from the ground the

Lord God caused to grow every tree that was pleasing to the sight and good for food, with the tree of life in the middle of the garden and the tree of knowledge of good and bad" (Gen. 2:9).

God's luck, not mine. Not only do weeds stubbornly reappear each season in places I thought I had rendered permanently weed-free, they also grow with such deceptive camouflage that sometimes even I, weed expert that I think I have become, cannot distinguish between plant stem and weed stalk. I hate to think about how many innocent obedient plant stems or monarda shoots I have mistakenly yanked up. The Master Gardener seems to have had none of these nagging little problems or, for that matter, problems of any kind. In Eden, a perfect biosphere was obtained, with God in full control: no aphids on the roses; no black spot; no weevils in the cotton; no borers in the Japanese black pines; the astilbes and the hostas planted in just the right parts of the shade; the garden in continuous bloom from April through October. Many mortals have come close to creating such a garden compleat. The landscape designers and those knowledgeable in plant material and the habit of plants at famous gardens such as Sissinghurst, Winterthur, Longwood Gardens, and the Brooklyn Botanic Garden, to name but a few, have created breathtakingly beautiful spaces, but none, I suspect, could compete with the Divinity's handiwork in Eden. Yet, strange as it may seem, God found that he did need help.

THE PARTNERSHIP

The Genesis story reveals a challenging truth: God could not maintain Eden alone.

No shrub of the field was yet on the earth and no grasses of the field had yet sprouted, because the Lord God had not sent rain upon the earth; and there was no man to till the ground.

Gen. 2:5

The Lord God took the man and placed him in the Garden of Eden to till it and tend it.

Gen. 2:15

Let us not underestimate the importance of these deceptively simple verses. The Bible is telling us that God needed human help so that the entire life/growth process might move forward.

The early rabbinic commentators jumped on this thought: "The edible fruits of the earth require not only God's gift of rain but also man's cultivation. Man must be a co-worker with God in making this earth a garden" (J. H. Hertz, ed., *Pentateuch and Haftorahs*). In other words, paradise was perfect — almost. It was complete — almost. For all its beauty, for all its wonderful design, something was missing. Us! God needed a partner: us.

One of Judaism's more audacious theological principles is that God and humanity need each other to complete the creative process. It is an empowering thought. Instead of seeing ourselves as yet another life form to be redeemed by some other, outside force, we see ourselves as essential, of intrinsic worth, possessed of such capacity that we are needed to complete the Eternal's plans for the universe. We may not be equal partners with God, but we are definitely part of the equation.

It is not much of an intellectual step to move from saying

that humans are of value to saying that they are unique —
qualitatively different from all other living things. The biblical
writers portrayed humans this way. In a highly imaginative
passage, they described our special relationship to God when
they wrote that we, more than any other living creature, possess the breath of God in our being. It was their way of saying
that they believed we have souls. "The Lord God formed man
of the dust of the earth. He blew into his nostrils the breath of
life, and man became a living soul" (Gen. 2:7).

Do cats and dogs and leopards and lizards also have
souls? Many pet lovers and animal rights activists swear that
they do. Perhaps so, but I doubt that anyone would argue that
the soul of a tadpole and the human spirit are qualitatively the
same. We have even enshrined this value judgment that the
one surpasses the other in our structure of law. It elevates
the value of human life above the value of any other living
thing. We give this value a name: sacred. Kill a bear or catch a
striped bass, and you may be fined. If the species is endan-
gered or under some other kind of special protection, you
may, at worst, be briefly imprisoned. But take the life of
another human being (except in a sanctioned situation such as
war or self-defense), and you risk the possibility of having the
state take yours. We have made a cardinal principle of the
concept that human beings are special, possessed of some
essence that positions them on the highest rung of the evolutionary ladder and thus subject to special protection. That is
why the Sixth Commandment is so explicit when it says
"Thou shalt not murder" rather than "Thou shalt not kill." The
biblical writers recognized the difference. We can kill in certain circumstances, but we cannot indiscriminately murder
each other without paying a terrible price in the courts of
justice.

So we see ourselves as unique. Fine, but uniqueness carries with it additional responsibilities.

THE BURDEN OF UNIQUENESS

We do not know how long the good life in Eden lasted for Adam and Eve, but we do learn that at one point, something seems to have gone terribly wrong. What brought Eden down? The answer is found in the following text: "And the Lord God commanded man, saying, 'Of every tree of the garden you are free to eat, but as for the tree of knowledge of good and bad, you must not eat'" (Gen. 2:17).

Why didn't God want Adam and Eve, the two best gardeners he ever had, to eat of the tree of knowledge? It is difficult to believe that God did not want human beings to be knowledgeable, informed, since the essence of humanity is our capacity to make informed choices. There had to be a different reason for restricting Adam and Eve from the tree of knowledge — a more compelling, more challenging reason.

God may have been testing Adam and Eve, testing their capacity for self-discipline. Even though they did not possess full knowledge, God had vested this first couple with free will. God had given them the capacity to choose between obedience and disobedience. And for whatever reason, they failed. They chose not to resist the temptation to eat the fruit. The biblical writers were trying to tell us something: From the very beginning, humans have had free will. It is a powerful tool. Use it wisely. People pay a price for poor choices.

Eve wanted to taste that apple, and so did Adam. The price they paid for that bite was steep, very steep indeed: expulsion from the garden. Thus was the course of human history forever changed. Of course, the snake took the rap for what happened, but truth be told, he was only a bit player in this scene. It was God, not the snake, who commanded the couple not to eat of the tree, and it was disobedience of that command that caused God to expel them from Eden. But that did not stop first- and second-century biblical commentators from tying the eviction to some illicit sexual awareness or from portraying the snake in negative and sexual terms. They got some help from the Bible, which tells us that "the serpent was the shrewdest of all the wild beasts that the Lord God had made" (Gen. 3:1). He talked. And he was defiant of God. One can almost hear him sidling up to Eve and, in the most seductively beguiling terms, hissing in her ear, "You are not going to die" (Gen. 3:4). It's little wonder that first-century Christian writers linked the snake to the Devil himself.

The *Apocalypse of Moses*, a Christian source written in Greek and dating from the first century, contains the following quote attributed to Eve: "The devil answered me through the mouth of the serpent." Another first-century Greek source, Maccabees, puts the matter erotically: "[A woman recalls] . . . nor did the Destroyer, the deceitful serpent, defile the purity of my virginity" (4 Macc. 18:7–8).

Here is the serpent as phallus. The phallus seen in negative, even hateful, terms. In fact, some religious traditions used the Eden story to link sex and sin. But there is no such connection in the biblical account. Other than a reference to nakedness — in and of itself not a sexually negative allusion — there is no sexual reference in the Garden of Eden story. Yet this harmful equation of sex and sinfulness persists to this very day, instilling in many people feelings of guilt about what are normal and healthy sexual feelings, and preventing social institutions such as schools and churches from talking openly and teaching honestly about human sexuality. Millions still cling to the belief that sex is in some ways "dirty" or, worse, sinful, requiring us to seek "purification" or "redemption" via some "holy," usually external, source. But it was not sex that caused Adam and Eve to be driven from the Garden of Eden. It was disobedience. Adam and Eve disobeyed a direct order from God not to eat of the tree of knowledge, and for that they were expelled. Herein lies the burden of their (and our) uniqueness: they had a choice, and they made the wrong one. Humanity's first sin was a wrongful use of its free will. The Eden story is not about sex; it is about disobedience and free will. That is the sum and substance of the story — no more, no less. The brilliant seventeenth-century English poet John Milton conveyed the true meaning of Eden when he wrote in *Paradise Lost*:

> . . . whose fault?
> Whose but his own? ingrate, he had of me
> All he could have; I made him just and right,
> Sufficient to have stood, though free to fall.
>
> .   .   .   .
> . . . they themselves decreed
> Their own revolt, not I.
>
> .   .   .   .
> They trespass, Authors to themselves in all
> Both what they judge and what they choose; for so
> I formed them free, and free they must remain,
> Till they enthrall themselves. . . .
>
> .   .   .   .
> . . . they themselves ordained their fall.

True, Adam and Eve were tempted, but they could have said no. That "could have" makes all the difference.

FREE WILL: THE PRICE
OF BEING HUMAN

Rational faith rests on the pillar of free will. Unless we are free to make choices in our lives, we are only puppets operating at the will of some other force, and we are not responsible for our behavior. We can blame someone or something else for what we do and for what happens to us. Many of Hitler's Nazis did just that. They claimed they were only following orders. The Allies did not buy their argument, and many of Hitler's minions were tried, imprisoned, or executed for their war crimes. History is full of examples of those who have tried to escape the consequences of their actions by claiming that they had no choice.

An even more dangerous consequence of the argument that we have no choice, that we are compelled by some out-side force such as God into a course of negative action, is that it makes of God a demonic, sometimes cruel Master Pup-peteer, responsible for people doing horrible things to one another. But we do have free will, and we must be responsible for our actions. One might question, then, what that view does to the idea that God is omnipotent (all-powerful) and omniscient (all-knowing). Do we not limit God's powers by so strongly insisting on free will and human choice?

Rabbi Akiba, a distinguished and oft-quoted first-century rabbi, understood the dilemma and responded, "Everything is seen, yet freedom is given." How can that be? we ask. Each of us, he continued, is born with a golden chain. One end of the chain is attached to our ankle, the other to a leg of the throne of God. But the chain is so long and so light that we never know we are on it.

Let me dramatize the point. Did God want the Holocaust? Does God really want any war? Is God some vengeful, bloodthirsty force that delights in people killing each other? Many people think that wars are inevitable. But would we want our political leaders and diplomats to stop negotiating for peace when conflict threatens? Of course not. We want to believe that human brains at work can resolve international tensions better than guns can. We want to believe that we are neither trapped nor doomed by the evil and hurt and pain that surround us and that we inflict on one another. We want to believe that we can shape what happens. It is faith, not fate, that shapes our lives — faith in ourselves and in our finer capacities. That is the kind of faith that makes sense.

There is a fascinating verse at the end of the Book of Deuteronomy. Moses is about to die. He stands before the people he has led for a generation, there to share with them for the last time the summation of all he has tried to teach them during the wilderness years. His words take on dramatic intensity: "I call heaven and earth to witness against you this day; I have put before you life and death, blessing and curse. Choose your life — if you and your offspring would live . . . for thereby you shall have life and shall long endure" (Deut. 30:19).

Choose life. It is in your hands, says Moses. What you choose will determine whether you continue or go out of existence as a people. Of course, what Moses wanted the people to choose were the ethical and ritual demands God had placed before them at Sinai, but he knew that God could not force the people of Israel to accept them. God had given the people choice. The people had the freedom to reject it all, and if any part of the biblical narrative is to be believed, they indeed did reject the demands as frequently as they accepted them. They worshiped false gods. They created places of worship, called high places, where sacred prostitution flourished. They left much to be desired in the way they conducted their business affairs. The writings of such prophets as Amos, Isaiah, and Jeremiah are replete with examples of Israel's bad choices. They explained that it was these decisions, not God's will to destroy the people, that resulted in their exile to Babylon by Nebuchadnezzar, its powerful warlord, after he captured Jerusalem and reduced the temple to smoking ruins.

CAIN AND ABEL: THE CHOICES THEY DID NOT MAKE

The Bible's early emphasis on humanity's free will appears again in the fratricidal tragedy found in chapter 4 of Genesis: the Cain and Abel story. No sooner were Adam and Eve out of the garden than Eve became pregnant — first with Cain and then with Abel. Never were there more mismatched brothers than these two.

"Abel became a keeper of sheep and Cain became a tiller of the soil" (Gen. 4:2). Enmity between farmer and shepherd is as old as human settlement. It is likely that this story of fraternal hate was included by the biblical writers to champion the rights of the shepherd over the rights of the farmer. The "school" that wrote this legend came from the southern mountainous section of ancient Canaan, where shepherding was the primary way of life and remained so until very recent times. As a young child living with my family for a year in what was then known as Palestine, I frequently saw herds of goats and sheep moving through the landscape of our community just south of Jerusalem. Shepherding was the way of life for the Bedouin who freely traveled that countryside.

The story of Cain and Abel is well known. They seem never to have lived in peace with each other. A ritual act brought matters to a head. Both offered sacrifices to their Deity. Abel's was accepted (the sign of that acceptance is not given us), Cain's rejected. Cain was furious.

God asked Cain, "Why are you angry?" (Gen. 4:6), as if the Eternal One did not know. But God did know, even as God probably knew what Cain was about to do. God did all that could be done to prevent what the Eternal saw coming.

> And the Lord said to Cain: why are you angry? And why is your face fallen? If you do well, shall it not be lifted up? And if you do not well, sin crouches at the door and unto you is its desire, *but thou mayest rule over it.*
>
> Gen. 4:7 *(italics added)*

The Hebrew words are *"v'atah timshal ba."* The construction of the language is telling.

Not only did the author John Steinbeck see the nuances here, but he built his entire novel *East of Eden* on understanding the powerful meaning of this fragment of conversation. Steinbeck rejected the translation of the phrase as found in the American Standard Version of the Bible — "Do thou rule over it" — which makes it an order, not what the text implies. Similarly, he rejected the King James translation of these words: "Thou shalt rule over him." This, he observed, is a promise that Cain would conquer sin. But the original text makes no such promise.

Steinbeck came to see the real meaning of the original Hebrew, and he put the explanation in the mouth of his character Lee, the Chinese cook and intellectual hero of *East of Eden:*

"Don't you see?" he cried. "The American Standard translation *orders* men to triumph over sin, and you can call sin ignorance. The King James translation makes a promise in 'Thou shalt,' meaning that men will surely triumph over sin. But the Hebrew word, the word *timshel* — 'Thou mayest' — that gives a choice. It might be the most important word in the world. That says the way is open. That throws it right back on a man. For if 'Thou mayest' — it is also true that 'Thou mayest not.' Don't you see?" . . .

". . . Now, there are many millions in their sects and churches who feel the order, 'Do thou,' and throw their weight into obedience. And there are millions more who feel predestination in 'Thou shalt.' Nothing they may do can interfere with what will be. But 'Thou mayest'! Why, that makes a man great, that gives him stature with the gods, for in his weakness and his filth and his murder of his brother he has still the great choice. He can choose his course and fight it through and win. . . . It cuts the feet from under weakness and cowardliness and laziness." . . .

". . . I feel that a man is a very important thing — maybe more important than a star. That is not theology. I have no bent toward gods. But I have a new love for that glittering instrument, the human soul. It is a lovely and unique thing in the universe. It is always attacked and never destroyed — because 'Thou mayest.'"

The use of the word *may* conveys exactly what the biblical writers wanted to say to their readers: we are given free will to choose the course of our behavior. Just imagine this exchange between God and Cain: "Cain! Whoa! Wait a minute. Think about what you are doing. You're angry now, but you don't have to kill Abel. Put down the weapon in your hand. Cool off a minute. Think it over. The sin of anger crouches at the door of your will. It tempts you, but wait, you can control it. You may rule over it. You are better than your present anger." That was all God could do or say.

Poor Cain! He probably could not even hear God at this moment. With adrenaline pumping through his entire being, maybe it was too much to expect Cain to step back. In any event, he didn't. With some instrument (the Bible does not tell us what kind), he killed Abel. God cried out, "Where is your brother? What have you done? Your brother's blood cries out to me" (Gen. 4:10). Immediately, Cain was overwhelmed with remorse and self-pity: "You have banished me this day from the soil and I must avoid your presence and become a restless wanderer on earth" (Gen. 4:14).

God and Cain no longer saw each other. Their faces were hidden from each other. How graphically accurate is this image. The moment we choose badly, act stupidly, hurt one another, we blind ourselves not only to one another but also to all that the word *Divinity* might mean in our lives.

THE IMPLICATIONS OF FREE WILL

The notion that God cannot command our moral choices is reflected through a well-known line found in the Talmud, Judaism's definitive postbiblical authority. There, in tractate Berakot 33b, we read that "everything is in the hands of God except the fear of God." By "fear" the writer meant respect for, not dread of.* The writer was exact. He wanted to convey the

---

*In Hebrew, the word for dread or terror is *pachad*, whereas the Hebrew word for respect or awe is a derivative of *yareh* — two different Hebrew words that convey two totally different feelings. In the passage quoted here, the latter word is used.

idea that God cannot force humanity to respect the Divinity or to follow God's wishes. People must freely choose to do that.

This is a remarkable thought, especially when one considers that it was written in the first century by men of great faith, who believed that God was both omniscient and omnipotent. There is also biblical precedent for it. In the wilderness, Moses rejected God's demand that he speak to the rock to bring water from it. Moses struck the rock instead (Num. 20). King Saul lost his throne because he chose to reject a divine commandment to totally destroy the Amalekites (1 Sam. 15). The Book of Jonah is the story of a man fleeing from God's explicit command to go to Nineveh and urge its citizens to repent. These incidents illustrate the idea that God cannot force people to do what God would like them to do. People must choose of their own free will. And they do, sometimes with disastrous consequences.

If we assume that God is all-knowing and wants what is best for us (there is an old saying, "If God is not good, he is not God"), how could God have allowed Hitler to destroy six million Jews in the Holocaust and twenty million people during World War II? How could God allow Serbs and Albanians to butcher each other in Kosovo? How could a God who we presume wants the best for humanity allow African tribes to slaughter one another in Uganda? How does God allow all the terrors that stalk our earth each day, sometimes perpetrated by individuals and institutions that have the temerity to call themselves religious?

Is there anyone anywhere in the world who has not asked himself or herself these questions, sometimes finding his or her inadequate response sufficient justification to abandon all forms of organized religion? Comments such as "It is God's will" or "It is in the hands of Allah" neither satisfy nor justify such actions.

Does God allow these tragedies to happen? Yes. Does God *want* them to happen? No.

Where was God at Auschwitz? One Jewish writer bitterly observed that during the Holocaust, God went up the chimneys of the crematoriums in the smoke of burning flesh. Such an answer only produces a sneer, and life cannot be lived by sneers. Cynicism does not answer the question, Where was God during this terrible time? There must be a response with which one can live and still find some meaning in a belief system that includes Divinity.

I believe that God cried at Auschwitz. What do I mean by that? Do I think God actually shed tears? Since I do not believe in an anthropomorphic God, one that possesses human qualities, I cannot mean that God literally cried. I speak metaphorically. Because we believe in a Divinity that is life-affirming, life-giving, life-enhancing, we can say only that God must have been deeply saddened — saddened to the point of tears when seeing the brutality that we chose to inflict on one another during this terrible time. Since God gave humanity the free will to act in whatever way it chose, God could not interfere. God could only silently witness and weep at the barbarity.

I believe that God cries wherever and whenever people selfishly and childishly choose to slaughter one another. God hates that behavior, but God cannot do anything about it. The moment God granted humanity free will was the moment God limited God's own self. God is finite. Does that sound like blasphemy? To some, yes. Not to me. My belief system must preserve free will, and I know that free will in some ways limits God. We have enormous knowledge at our command.

We know a lot about how our universe functions. That knowledge allows us to put people on the moon, or in orbit, or on space stations. Because most of this knowledge is so technical, we tend to ignore much of it, often preferring instead to live by preconceived ideas, some of which are at wide variance with the truths our new knowledge has given us. That causes some problems, which I will discuss later on when I write about the modern dilemmas science poses for religion (see chapter 6).

We know how to make things grow better now than ever before in the history of the world. We can and do greatly enhance the nutritional value of food. We know how to grow more in less space. We can improve the breeding of living creatures used for food. In fact, we have created a situation in which no one in the world needs to go hungry. If people starve (and millions do), it is for political reasons and not because we have not learned how to make more and better food available. For reasons that upon examination often seem as cruel as they are bizarre and irrational, we have chosen not to exercise our more humane options.

No gardener would ever permit his or her garden to get so far out of balance, so totally discordant, as we have allowed the world to become in matters of food distribution and elementary well-being. A garden is a world in microcosm. For either to flourish, greed needs to be rooted out, whether it comes from a too-powerful weed, a rampant plant in a garden, or a ruler or political system that, in order to accumulate wealth, ignores the poor and hungry of its population. A beautiful garden is an ecologically balanced place, where sunlight, moisture, insects, plants, and birds all have specifically interdependent roles to play. When one gets out of balance, the entire space suffers. The gardener's job is to maintain that

God-given balance. Considering the many hostile forces unconsciously at work to destroy that balance, it is amazing that we have as many wonderful garden spaces as we do. The parallel with the world today is obvious.

We know what individuals and societies need to stay alive, to grow, to live in peace. We know, for example, that a grossly unequal distribution of goods and wealth in a community will give rise to discontent, jealousy, and a struggle to redress the imbalance by those who feel deprived. It is in our self-interest as individuals and as people in a community to see that the necessary resources, food, shelter, and work, which give individuals a sense of self-worth, are available to all. There will always be those who have more and those who have less, but we have learned that we cannot accept a situation in which too few have too much and too many have too little. Such a situation breeds discontent and enmity. We know that greed can eventually destroy us and our environment. We can choose to create social situations in which economic equity becomes the norm and greed is controlled. When we permit one society to sink into poverty, we create a situation that is ripe for the rise of one who promises to "save" the people and restore their former glory. Hitler might never have come to power had Germany not been destroyed economically after its 1918 military defeat. America went through a similar challenge during the Great Depression in the early 1930s. Only a democratic process that brought to power a government that understood the needs of an economically and socially sick America saved it from chaos and disaster.

Similarly, the choices we make as individuals — be they in life partners, vocations, the number of children we sire, the educational routes we pursue or ignore — all determine whether our lives are miserable or joyous. Our present and our future are in our own hands.

So where does all this leave God?

When things go wrong, we have a tendency to blame God. But God deserves more and better from us. We know, or at least by now we should know, that God is not responsible for the disasters we create by our own poor social choices. We cannot blame God for our apparent unwillingness to tackle the problems of our inner cities or to improve public education by committing the resources needed for better schools and teachers. We cannot blame God for the human greed that has created and allows to continue the environmental and atmospheric destruction now occurring worldwide, affecting our air, our oceans, and our very lives.

It is we who have made these poor choices. As we do, and because God gave us free will to make these choices, all God can do is weep. This is what I meant by a finite God. God is self-limited. God cannot, on the one hand, grant humanity free will and, on the other hand, interfere every time we make a bad choice. God has restricted God's own power to interfere. The situation is analogous to a child with a parent. At some point in a child's development, the parent has to let the child make his or her own choices. As parents, all we can do is hope and pray that what we have given our children in terms of training, love, and guidance will positively influence their decisions. When the choices are wrong, even as we might have foreseen, all we can do is be there to pick up the pieces, extend our love, reassure, comfort, and keep on going. My father (may he rest in peace) would regularly tell me, especially at moments when I had made a really stupid choice, "I cannot put my head on your shoulders."

We need constantly to remind ourselves that in the realm of social relationships, God does not *do*. God *is*. *We* do.

What we do makes the difference between whether God is expressed or denied in the world. We are the recipients of a tremendous gift, a great garden: earth and its environments. We are placed in the middle of it. We are also the recipients of a great responsibility: to use our free will. What shall we plant? Where shall we plant it? What shall we move or remove? What shall we harvest? We make the choices. God watches. God waits. And above all, God hopes.

CHAPTER II

Coneflowers and Sex

(i do not know what it is about you that closes
and opens; only something in me understands
the voice of your eyes is deeper than all roses)
nobody, not even the rain, has such small hands

E. E. Cummings, "somewhere i have
never travelled, gladly beyond"

I n chapter 1, I dismissed the idea that somehow the human sex drive — seen by some as evil and used by Eve to seduce Adam — motivated God to drive them from paradise. Still, there is no denying that because of the deliberate misreading of this ancient tale, sex and sin have been linked — a linkage that has caused grief, pain, and guilt to untold generations of faithful believers who, because they were and are human, persist in "doing what comes naturally," precisely because it is natural (and good).

Nothing is more basic to life than sex. And here humanity and nature mirror each other. Gardening is also about sex,
reproduction, proliferation. All one has to do is watch what
goes on out there in the backyard to realize just how sexual
nature is. That may seem a rather romantic way of putting it,
but reproduction is surely at the very heart of gardening. It
goes on all the time, right under our noses, whether we are
watching or not, and thank God for that.

Anyone who has ever planted mint or laid down a patch
of ajuga or lamium for a ground cover knows exactly what I
mean. They are incredible, almost unstoppable, spreaders. I
learned a trick about cultivating mint a long time ago. Unless
you want it to take over your garden, be very certain that you
place each sprig of mint in a plastic container before you plant
it. This will keep it from spreading through an entire area.
While ajuga makes a lovely ground cover with its dark purple
foliage and small, blue, spiky flower heads, it can invade a
lawn or garden bed before you put your shovel away for the
season. I once planted lamium near a bed of spring-blooming
columbines, but the lamium was so invasive that within two
years, it killed the columbines. I ended up redigging the entire
bed to eliminate the lamium and invested a small fortune in a
new order of columbine.

Echinacea, commonly known as coneflower, is a standard in the repertoire of any perennial garden, and for good
reason. Part of the daisy family, coneflowers are large, bright,
long-lasting flowers on tall stems that first appear in midsum-
mer and bloom until frost. Their petals range in color from
lovely magenta to white, and their centers are bright black
rounds of seeds. In the fall, as the plants begin to die, the wind
scatters the seeds from their summer nests, peppering the garden. The following spring, young seedling plants show up all

over the garden. Clearly, coneflowers' casual, somewhat irresponsible propagative behavior can get out of hand. (One of the nice things about coneflowers, however, is that they are a natural antibiotic, used by those who practice folk medicine. I'll talk about this further in chapter 9.)

What is true of plants such as coneflowers, mint, lamium, and ajuga is true of many perennials. A gardener soon learns that while sex in the garden is necessary, simple, and beautiful, reproduction cannot be allowed to become excessive if a garden is to be balanced. Without careful monitoring, a plant population can get uncontrollably rowdy, with the larger, tougher plants crowding out and eventually killing off the more tender, weaker ones. Left alone or ignored, a garden will eventually succumb to its bully boys, weeds and wild grasses, which will soon take over and destroy it. The wise gardener learns that a beautiful garden depends on controlled reproduction.

SEX AND RELIGION

Reproduction in a garden is so natural, so easy, so free and innocent, that one wonders why it can't be like that among people. True, we know that there are no moral values associated with reproduction in nature. But as we see what is happening sexually throughout the world, one has to wonder whether the moral strictures about sex and reproduction that we have tried to impose on people, many of whom come from cultures far older and more sophisticated than ours, are as legitimate, as moral, or as correct as we think they are.

Moreover, we have reason to be troubled by the reality that even in this day and age, something so fundamental and enjoyable as reproduction and sex should be weighed down by as much misinformation, secrecy, guilt, and shame as it seems to be. How did this happen? What chain of events, what teachings, what attitudinal prejudices have brought us to our present state of affairs, and what, if anything, can and should we do about this?

Religion must bear some of the burden for these attitudes. Historically, religion has been the prime shaper of our sexual beliefs. As we have already seen in chapter 1, this probably started with the earliest interpretations of the Adam and Eve story, in which Eve is portrayed as a sex object, a temptress, a seducer. Her temptation of Adam was mixed into a theological stew that seemed to say that sex was at best a necessary evil. Some people still love to quote Paul: "Better to marry than to burn" (1 Cor. 7:9). What a view of marriage!

Early Christianity made a sharp distinction between two kinds of love — physical and spiritual. The first was called eros, the second agape, which was equated with spiritual love, not of the body. The goal seemed to be to separate love from sex. Why? Early Christians saw eros, or the sex act, as defiling; intercourse was the way "sin" was transmitted from one generation to the next, thus making necessary the redemptive power of Christ's grace. Agape, on the other hand, was pure and holy, and should not be defiled by eros. One cannot help thinking that even today, one of the reasons so many people are troubled by sex is that their religion still either teaches them or allows them to feel guilty about their natural sexual urges, still equating them with that old theological dichotomy.

Judaism makes no such distinction. Sex and love are indissolubly linked, the one leading to the other. The Hebrew word for love, *ahavah*, is used to describe both its physical and

its spiritual components. Sexual desire is a normal, healthy by-
product of love; neither should cause guilt or shame. Jewish
religious literature is frank and outspoken when dealing with
the sexual aspect of the human experience. It is neither prud-
ish nor pornographic. No finer example of this can be found
than the words of the biblical writer of the Song of Songs, one
of the Bible's most erotic and spiritually beautiful texts. The
writer sees God as the Master Gardener, and everything in the
world of nature becomes a metaphor for human love:

> How fair and how pleasant art thou,
> O love, for delights!
> This thy stature is like a palm tree
> And thy breasts two clusters of grapes
> I said I will climb into the palm tree.
> I will take hold of the branches thereof;
> And let thy breasts be as clusters of the vine
> And the smell of thy countenance like apples;
> And your kisses like the best wine,
> that glideth down smoothly for my beloved.
> Moving gently the lips of those that are asleep.
> I am my beloved's and his desire is toward me.
> Come, my beloved, let us go forth into the field.
>
> *Song of Songs 7:6–11*

Some have tried to suggest that this is metaphorical writing
describing the relationship of God to the people of Israel. But
it seems clear that the words describe physical love between a
man and a woman. Imagine what must have gone through the
minds of those who two thousand years ago had to decide
whether to include this passionate, erotic book in the biblical
canon. Obviously, there were no censorship committees in
those days.

Postbiblical literature reflects the same view of sex. The Talmud teaches, "When a man and a woman unite with mutual love and desire, the Divine Presence abides with them" (Babylonian Talmud, Sota, 17a). Judaism sees the sex act as "worthy, good, and beneficial even to the soul. No other human activity can compare with it. There is nothing impure or defective about it, rather there is much exaltation" (Rabbi Jacob Emden Mor Ukeziah, No. 240).

One of the most moving affirmations of this is found in the writings of a distinguished Spanish Jewish philosopher, Moses ben Nahman Gerondi, more commonly known as Nachmanides (1194–1270):

> We believe that God, blessed be He, created . . . nothing containing obscenity or ugliness. . . . For if we were to say that intercourse is obscene, it would follow that the sexual organs are obscene. . . . And how could God . . . create something containing a blemish or obscenity, or a defect; for we would find that His deeds are not perfect, though Moses the greatest of the prophets proclaims, "The Rock, whose work is perfect" (Deut. 32:4). . . . He created man and woman, fashioning all their organs and setting them in their proper function, with nothing obscene about them. (Quoted in Charles B. Chavel, *Kitvei Rabbenu Moshe ben Nahman*, Jerusalem, 1964)

Was Nachmanides some radical for his age? Not at all. He was simply restating the normative thinking of his community, living as he did in the midst of a larger, dominant, and sometimes tyrannical religious Christian world with a totally different view of sexual matters.

Furthermore, Judaism teaches that sexual intercourse is entered into for reasons other than reproduction, that it is for pleasure and for pleasuring, an aspect of sex unique to humans. Animals mate. For them, the act is quick, joyless, impersonal. How different we can be from animals, and what a pity that all too often we copulate only like them.

SEX AND LOVE

We need to help one another understand that there is more to sexuality than orgasm, that we can take our pleasuring capacity and refine it, elevating it to a level no animal will ever experience. People today are beginning to realize this, and some are even beginning to accept the possibility that such experiences can be entered into and enjoyed outside of marriage, in serious, long-term, monogamous relationships. When asked whether a relationship between unmarried people is permitted, Nachmanides responded, "I do not know why there is any cause for doubt, for of course she is permitted to him since she lives with him. . . . If she comes into his house and lives with him and is known to him . . . she is permitted" (Responsa of Nachmanides, No. 2).

Marriage does not legitimize sex. Sex sacralizes marriage. Sex is a way — when we are young, probably the most powerful way — we choose to say "I love you, I want you to have all of me, and in the giving, I want to take all of you into my being, to hold, to cherish, to totally share all I am and have." As we grow older and physical desire slackens, we develop and use other skills to express these enormous emotions — words, gifts, shows of affection or concern — but youth is the age for sexual expression. That is why I believe that the young need to learn everything there is to know about sex. All people, adults as well as adolescents, need the mysteries of human sexuality removed so its essential truth may emerge.

We need to know about the mechanics of sex and reproduction to be able to appreciate its wonder and to be capable of the responsible use of this powerful, sometimes overpowering demand of body and mind. It is hard enough to teach this under the best of circumstances, but impossible to convey under circumstances of denial, fear, lack of information, or misinformation. What we also need to know is that sex can be a lethal weapon, one that a person can use to hurt and punish another. A young male, stimulated and engorged with raging testosterone and confronting a female of his sexual choice who may not wish to deal with his urges, is usually not in an equal-opportunity situation. Nor is it a learning time. The two people should be educated before so that when that moment arises, they can make an informed decision. Sex can be, and for most of us is, enjoyable and satisfying. It also can be very dangerous. It can make us sick, it can change our lives, and it can kill us. People need to know that.

Contraception is a critical part of this learning. Judaism is unequivocally clear in its advocacy of the use of birth control. The Talmud, Judaism's definitive rabbinic guide, states that at least three types of women are permitted to use a device to prevent conception: a minor, a pregnant woman, and a nursing mother. The subject is dealt with no fewer than six times in the Talmud, making it clear that there is no real religious objection to the use of mechanical or chemical contraception. Jews understand this quite well, and it is not an issue in contemporary Jewish life. In fact, it has been said, with levity but also with seriousness, that Jews are the best practitioners of birth control in the world. Some Orthodox Jews may oppose the use of birth control not because they fail to find religious sanction for it, but because they choose to have large families as a repudiation of the Holocaust and the near extermination of European Jewish life under Nazism.

A more open, more honest understanding of sexual matters could make a difference for America. That is why I believe that everyone, young and old, needs to know about and have inexpensive, easy access to safe, effective contraception. Without this, the garden of life may soon be overrun and overpopulated.

SEX AS A POLITICAL ISSUE

Clearly, issues surrounding human reproduction are now contorting this country's (and the world's) social and political scenes. In America, it is not just reproduction that troubles us; it is sex itself, which continues to tantalize us. Despite the fact that modern Christian teachings are trying to get away from the old beliefs that sex is "wrong" or "dirty," the old mythology seems to have a strong survival factor that is reflected in the schizophrenic way we view sex.

On the one hand, we seem to be eager to be entertained blatantly by sex, while on the other hand, we repress or deny its existence in other aspects of our social, religious, and educational lives. Sex enthralls us in our movies, on our TV and computer screens, in our jokes, in our social behavior, in much of our literature, in the way we are enticed into buying products. At some level, we seem not to be able to get enough of it. But we resist having too much of it taught in our public schools, and many of us are reluctant to raise the topic with our children or to respond honestly and intelligently to their queries. Most religious institutions shun discussing or teaching about sex except in the most bland or negative terms. Abortion and women's rights to reproductive health are the most divisive issues in American social politics, evoking the most irrational emotional responses and such inflamed passions that people are murdered over them.

But this is not just an American social debate. The world is seriously threatened by a population explosion and a resulting world overpopulation. This situation will not go away, no matter how much we refuse to look at it or deal with it. And it is not just "there," wherever "there" might be — China, Africa, South America? It is here in our own communities.

A DARKENING CLOUD

Twenty years ago, when I turned the first piece of sod for the first bed of what was then going to be a small garden, no houses bracketed my acreage. A family of pheasants occupied the woods on one side of the house, and the remains of a nineteenth-century apple orchard filled the other. Every fall, the deer would enter that old orchard to feast on the apples I did not or could not pick. Now deer are not my favorite friends. In fact, I do not like them at all. They can eat down a garden in a night, ruining months of work, but I did love watching them in that orchard, on their hind legs, stretching for the uppermost of the crop in the highest branches.

Today houses abut both sides of that house. In the past two decades, fifteen new large, single-occupancy homes have been built, filling the previously empty space that once surrounded me with its silent beauty. The pheasants are gone, the orchard leveled (a large house has replaced it). Sprawl is the name of the latest builders' game. Only it is no game. It is a deadly blight in many parts of America, even as our urban cores rot for lack of decent low-income housing.

Housing for an increasingly overpopulated world is an endemic problem, a social consequence of the population explosion, a by-product of uncontrolled human sexuality. Those who argue that the earth can sustain an unlimited number of people and that all we need to do is grow crops more efficiently and then effectively distribute what we grow — so that those now starving or living at subsistence levels will have better access to them and thus live happier, more rewarding lives — may be right. But their dreams are in danger of being overrun by the reality of overpopulation before these systems of worldwide production and distribution can be put in place to justify their faith in those plans. The world's population will soon reach eight billion — four times what it was in 1926, my birth year. Most of the growth is occurring in the world's most impoverished areas — places where life expectancy is at its lowest, where levels of illiteracy and lack of skills are at their highest, and where primary health care is woefully inadequate.

Such realities should give one pause to consider whether we approach sex in the right or best way. Certainly, sex has polarized our political and social views of one another here and throughout the world. If only we could take Candide's famous advice to just cultivate our own gardens. But we cannot. The dilemmas of the rest of the world impinge on our private lives no matter how hard we try to keep them out.

MARRIAGE AND GARDENS

One day some years ago, on a late-summer afternoon after a particularly vigorous, very hot day in the garden, I stood still for a minute just to admire the space. It was, I confess, a most satisfying moment. The coneflowers were a chorus. The honeybees were rummaging deeply in the red monarda patch. The blue veronica spikes rising in front of the bee balm contrasted perfectly with the red behind them. The white loosestrife blended with the yellow of the ligularia growing in front of it. All the colors meshed. All the elements of the garden seemed to be in perfect relationship, almost as though they were married. Even the little stream that sneaks through a back corner of the yard was doing its merry thing with a quiet gurgle. Altogether, it was a moment as glorious as it was rare — the kind of moment that gardeners break their backs for and that makes gardening so worthwhile and satisfying.

Married! Marriage. I leaned on my shovel and started thinking.

A week earlier, I had met for the first time with a couple who had come to my study for a routine prewedding interview. Never had I seen two people less suited for each other. They seemed to have nothing in common. Nothing matched in their lives. There was no blending of color on any level. Yet they professed their mutual love. What is love? How long could their chemistry last? What about the absence of compatibility in religion, education, and temperament that so clearly emerged as we talked? I remembered some advice my father, who was also a rabbi, once gave me: "The only thing that should be different about two people wanting to get married should be their sex." OK, maybe a bit glib and not totally descriptive for today's needs, but Dad had something.

Reverting to my gardening analogy, the greater the harmony and the more the materials blend and complement one another, the more satisfying is the garden. That surely applies equally to marriage. The more interests a couple share — beyond the orgasmic, important as that is — the better their chances of having a successful, permanent relationship. As every garden is constantly subject to pests, so is every relationship subject to stresses that can shatter it. Without strong similarities of interest, background, culture, the chances of its survival are jeopardized.

Much as we all love good sex, it really is not enough by itself. Love and sex deserve much more. To cultivate sex and think it is love, or to sanctify some nonphysical love and deny or denigrate sex, is to create an imbalance that can, and frequently does, lead to unhappiness between two people. I remember once quipping to my sons, then young men, "Guys, never mix up your sex lives and your love lives."

What I intended to suggest was that recreational sex engaged in by mutual consent and practiced safely is natural and understandable, but they should not mistake it for love. Real love suggests something far more serious: establishing a permanent relationship with someone, building a home, creating a family. These are tough, hopefully long-term, goals, and they require mutual decisions to be made seriously, rather than being entered into casually.

CHANGING SEXUAL
AND SOCIAL MORES

The Jewish community has historically had a reputation for family preservation. Divorce, while allowed, until recently was not an action taken with great frequency. Yet we know that our families are not immune from unhappy and dysfunctional marriages. Abuse and abandonment also exist in Jewish family life, and we have not escaped the corrosive effects on family that changing social mores have had. The breakdown of the nuclear family has brought rising divorce rates to Jewish life, as it has to all other cultures. Our social service agencies and professionals must deal with an increase in various types of abusive situations. Family is no longer defined in traditional terms, but that does not mean that people are not seeking family. If divorce is on the increase, so is remarriage. New styles of permanent relationships are emerging, as is a greater tolerance of such nontraditional relationships. We are learning, albeit slowly — and for some, not without much kicking and screaming — that gay and lesbian couples can have families as functional as those of heterosexuals and ought to be allowed to do so.

Opponents of the gay lifestyle love to quote Scripture to justify their opposition, and clearly the scripture is there to quote: "Thou shall not lie with a man as with a woman: it is an abomination" (Lev. 18:22). Nothing could be more clear. In fact, it is a crime punishable by death. But then so is adultery in the Bible, and when was the last time an American court condemned someone to death for that "crime"? The biblical attitude finds its corollary in the New Testament. Paul, in his Epistle to the Romans, excoriates same-sex relationships as "dishonorable" and "unnatural" (Rom. 1:26–27). Subsequent interpreters of Christianity only reinforced the revulsion against homosexuality.

What has caused the contemporary change in attitude? There are probably many factors, but the general weakening of traditional religion has surely diminished the influence of religious teaching on the people of this country. And with so many new and different lifestyles in abundance, advocates of gay rights argue with increasing potency that they, too, are entitled to practice what they consider to be their equally legitimate lifestyle. Nations such as France, England, Italy, Sweden, Denmark, Switzerland, Mexico, Uruguay, and Canada have decriminalized homosexuality.

What, then, should be the attitude of modern, non-orthodox religionists toward this difficult issue? We find a powerful instruction in the pages of the Talmud. We are taught: "You have to judge according to that which you see with your own eyes" (Baba Bathra, 43a).

I, like most clergy, have seen with my own eyes and heard with my own ears the cries of homosexuals. They have come into my study to speak with me, to pour out their hearts to me. Why me? Because I am a rabbi, one who will listen. What do they want of me? Absolution? Protection? Assurance? None of these. They come to me because they want to be with someone who can hear them as they say, "I have not chosen my sexual orientation or lifestyle. This is not a matter of sexual preference. It has been for me a living hell. I no more chose my attachment to another of my own gender than you, Rabbi, chose the love of a woman." A colleague of mine, Rabbi Jerome Davidson, once observed:

> Increasingly we know that homosexuality is as involuntary and determined as heterosexuality. It is not a willed choice, an ideological commitment. It is a powerful involuntary attraction, as [psychiatrist Dr. Harry Stack] Sullivan puts it, "bound up in the mysterious and unstable area where sex and desire and emotional longing meet; it reaches into the core of what makes a human being who he or she is."

Homosexuality is not a choice. It is not a matter of controlling one's instincts or urges. Rabbi Harold Schulweis shares this empathetic view:

> The underlying issue is moral not textual. . . . We cannot, as thinking, feeling Jews, base our judgment solely on a verse or two in the Bible.

What is required of us is to accept the dignity of each individual, to know the hearts of these strangers, to make them feel at home with us and to encourage them to live out their lives with dignity and within compassionate communities. . . . Every human being is created in God's image. . . . To humiliate God's creations is to spit in God's face. . . . That is an abomination we can cleanse from our midst. ("A Second Look at Homosexuality," *Tikkun*, vol. 12, no. 3)

We can meld nature with our own human nature, learn to live with and ensure acceptance for those who for reasons known only to God live their sexual lives differently from most people.

Let's look again at the beautiful melding of nature and human sexuality in the Song of Songs:

I am a rose of Sharon
A lily of the valleys.
Like a lily among thorns
So is my darling among the maidens.
Like an apple tree among the trees of the forest
So is my beloved among the youth.
In his shade I delight to sit
And his fruit is sweet in my mouth.

.   .   .   .

My beloved is mine, and I am his, who browses among the
    lilies.

.   .   .   .

Blow upon my garden,
That its perfume may spread,
Let my beloved come into his garden
And enjoy its luscious fruits.

.   .   .   .

Eat, O lovers and drink:
Drink deep of love.

Song of Songs 2:1–5:1

The Song of Songs spiritualizes both sexuality and nature by joining them together. The one fulfills the other without artificial distinctions. This is the way life really ought to be — the conscious awareness that the person opposite you in any sexual encounter possesses sanctity. A sexual partner is created in the spiritual image of Divinity, a person to be held as sacrosanct as you hold your own life. That person ought not to be trivialized or used, overpowered or trashed. His or her feelings, emotions, physical and spiritual sensitivities need to be as carefully and as slowly cultivated as you would cultivate the coneflowers in your garden.

It is autumn as I write this chapter. Autumn is a busy season for gardeners. There are leaves to be raked up and disposed of around the garden, bulbs to be planted, plants and shrubs to be moved to the better locales we staked out during the summer, and nurseries to be prowled. Many of them are in the middle of their fall sales. They do not want to store their unsold stock over the winter. Careful hunting can turn up some wonderful bargains.

Fall is also a time to keep promises. Gardeners are a promising, swapping band. Earlier in the spring, I promised to give a friend and fellow gardener two sections from plants in my garden: a piece of a spring-blooming pulmonaria and a section of a large euphorbia, also known as spurge, that has been growing unmolested for five years. In return, she has given me some rhizomes from a special Dutch iris she has that

I truly covet. (Irises need to be divided every three or four years.) She has left those rhizomes on my deck. Now it is pay-back time. My shovel bites into the pulmonaria. One quick slice and voilà, she has her plant. The euphorbia does not yield as gracefully. Beautiful as it is in the spring with its brilliant chartreuse flowers, euphorbia grows large in circumference and develops a tough root system after a few years. Cutting through the mass of roots is a difficult, muscle-using process. Done.

Next spring, two beautiful new plants will burst forth in all their glory. They will never know they were divided. Next spring, some of me will be in my friend's garden and vice versa. We are connected: a satisfying thought. How easily a garden reproduces: "O Lord, our God, how excellent is thy name in all the earth" (Ps. 8:9).

When the Rhododendron Died

The true motivation for prayer is not, as it has been said, the sense of being at home in the universe, but rather the sense of not being at home in the universe. . . . To pray means to bring God back into the world. . . .

Abraham Joshua Heschel,
The Insecurity of Freedom

*T*he life and eventual demise of one of the most beautiful rhododendrons I have ever grown helped me understand some important values about prayer — its purpose, what we can and what we should not expect prayer to accomplish, and how we can avoid the kind of disappointment we feel when what we pray for is not realized.

The commercial name of this spectacular plant is 'Scintillation'. This is not a rare variety, but it is somewhat uncommon, and not every nursery will carry it. The flower it produces is a rich pink with a deep magenta, almost purple, throat. Its truss (the width of the blossom) is three to five inches — smaller than the blooms of a tree peony, but still impressive. A mature plant can grow five or six feet high and will span almost as much in diameter. When it is in bloom in late May or early June (depending on locale, climate, and growing conditions), the blossoms cover the entire plant — a breathtaking spectacle. Clearly, 'Scintillation' is not your ordinary plant.

Our friend Nat had given us a medium-size one from his personal stock. As a licensed hybridizer, he has cultivated many unusual varieties of rhododendrons. In its prime, his personal garden on Long Island was a blazing fairyland during the spring months, and people came from all over to walk through the seven or more acres.

We were living in Manhattan at the time, and our apartment had a large terrace garden that didn't get much sun because of the buildings surrounding it. This is the perfect condition for rhododendrons, essentially forest plants that thrive in shade. Since terrace gardeners must plant everything in planters or containers, our 'Scintillation' began her urban life in an old whiskey tub into which I had first mixed massive amounts of humus, leaf mold, peat moss, and vermiculite — all the right things to give the plant a good start. (That soil looked and smelled so good to me that I almost thought I could have it for lunch.) The plant is somewhat shallow-rooted, so its root ball fit nicely into the tub, with plenty of room for a Styrofoam liner around the inside. Fierce winter winds, freezing rain, and the most miserable wet snow — typical of New York winters — were a constant threat, as were the devilish February thaws, when the temperature might soar to 40 or 50 degrees Fahrenheit one day and plunge to below freezing the next. Plants do not like such wild temperature variations. For protection, I wrapped the "rhody" in burlap.

I was determined to give the new arrival the best possible care, and she got it: springtime fertilization, fall feedings of bonemeal, a winter spraying of the leaves with an antidesiccant to prevent them from drying out, and summer waterings. 'Scintillation' was loved, pampered, worried about, nurtured, and she responded in kind, unfolding her pink treasures on our terrace for eight springs. During the two last weeks of May, she would shamelessly parade her beauty, a brazen pink hussy reveling in her abandon. Since the terrace was on the second floor of the building, neighbors above were able to enjoy her as much as we did. In the elevator, residents who might never have even said hello asked about her health and welfare, advised us on her care. A few would occasionally even lean out their windows to ask if perhaps I could cut a small branch of blossoms for them, as they were having a dinner party, and wouldn't it be nice if . . . We would try to oblige, especially since selective pruning is good for the plant.

The years passed, and even after 'Scintillation' shed her pink plumage for a rich burst of green new growth, she continued to dominate the garden. Other plants — some perennial, some annual — would come and go, but she reigned as a queen should: majestically, quietly, overarching without being overbearing.

I do not remember the exact moment I noticed the first leaf drop, although I do remember being mildly concerned. That summer, instead of the expected new growth and bud formation, the leaves at the bottom of the plant turned yellow and dropped. My anxiety grew, but after all, the plant was getting older, she lived in a tough environment, and it was natural for a few leaves to die. Then matters grew worse that fall. About a third of her leaves carpeted the terrace floor, and by February a pruning of some of her dead outer branches showed the extent of her illness. Instead of being green in the core of the branches, it was brown — in short, dead. All that winter, I watched the plant's branches turn naked against the winter drear as her long leaves fell from the dying wood. I was reminded of a line from a Shakespeare sonnet: "bare ruined choirs, where late the sweet birds sang."

That spring, there was no bud break. In fact, 'Scintillation' never bloomed again. She died in late March. In April, I dug her out of the whiskey tub and sawed her main trunk in half to see if I could discover the cause of her death. A borer had entered her trunk. I could see the tiny holes. It had then slowly sapped the life juices out of the plant as they tried to rise from root to stem each spring. I cut her into small pieces, stuffed them into a black garbage bag, and dragged it all down to the curb. The Department of Sanitation truck geared down in front of our apartment building about six the next morning. I know because I was wide-awake — sick at heart and angry. The grinding of the truck's mechanism assaulted me as the plastic coffin was quite unceremoniously heaved into the truck's rear maw. The truck moved quickly down the street to the next pile of detritus, and then — the silence of early morning in Manhattan.

Damn! Damn! I thought. I could feel my grief turning to palpable anger. Then I began to remember phrases, outbursts I had heard from people who had lost someone, usually after a prolonged illness during which much personal care had been administered. Their outbursts were really not directed toward me. I was just the closest listener at the moment of their pain. I could hear their laments ringing in my ears: After all I did for her. After all the love I showered on her. How dare she die on me? It isn't fair. She should have lived a lot longer. Where is the justice? My thoughts drifted back to my lost 'Scintillation'. So maybe she was only a plant, but, my God, she was also a living thing. Isn't God supposed to be as concerned for the sparrow as for the saint? Everything seemed to be in the hands of a mindless, cruel fate — the luck of the draw, and my draw was bad. *To hell with the plant. God doesn't care. Tomorrow I will go to a nursery and find another rhody. It won't be 'Scintillation', but it will fill up the tub, and that will be enough.* I was bitter. I cried for the loss of my beautiful plant.

DEATH AND UNANSWERED PRAYERS

As I sat in my study that early morning, my professional life began to crowd in on me. The death of the plant was indeed a metaphor. I began to remember how many times I had heard people express these same feelings when, in frustration and grief over the death of a loved one, they would turn on God angrily: How could God have let my husband die? What did I do to deserve this? God knows I prayed enough. Where is God when we need him? What is the point of prayers?

When I first began my rabbinate, I tried to answer such complaints. After all, I thought, these were basically theological questions, ones I saw as attacking the very foundations of my belief system. I was threatened by them and felt they deserved hard theological responses. I would try to reason with people: God is not cruel. God did not single out your husband and take his life just to punish you. Besides, God is not some "cosmic bellhop" waiting to respond to your personal prayer button when you decide to push it.

I soon learned that I was wasting my time. The questions people ask in moments of extreme duress do not usually call for answers. They are, rather, cries of the heart, a venting of despair, an expression of sadness as a person confronts the ultimacy of physical death. I learned that instead of delivering a theological lecture, the best thing I could do was put my arm around the person, share with him or her the warmth of my caring heart, and let the person know that I felt his or her pain. I realized that it was important to empathize, not moralize; to embrace, not try to justify; to love, not lecture. These truths are powerfully expressed in an incisive homily titled "For a Time of Sorrow" by the distinguished theologian and poet Howard Thurman:

> I share with you the agony of your grief,
> The anguish of your heart finds echo in my own.
> I know I cannot enter all you feel
> Nor bear with you the burden of your pain;
> I can but offer what my love does give:
> The strength of caring,
> The warmth of one who seeks to understand
> The silent storm-swept barrenness of so great a loss.
> This I do in quiet ways,
> That on your lonely path
> You may not walk alone.

I saw that this was the best response to the immediacy of death, but there came a time later when the questions of the bereaved did indeed need to be dealt with — a time when a person's legitimate curiosity about the place of Divinity in our affairs deserved reasoned responses: Does God get involved in the affairs of individuals? Is it legitimate to pray for a person's life as he or she lies hovering at death's door? What prayers are acceptable when someone we love is sick or in trouble? Does God actually hear prayers or answer them?

THE PURPOSE OF PRAYER

My father, an eminent American rabbi, once gave this definition of prayer: "For me prayer has become meditation upon the best we know, communion with the noblest that we understand, and reaching out of what we are to what we yearn to be."

I like that definition because it completely shifts the grounds of responsibility from God to us. It reverses the common view that in prayer, we should somehow affect God, compelling the Eternal One to do something for us. Not so, my father suggested. God is an ideal, a paradigm of all we hold of ultimate value or good. Prayer is the activity we enter into to enable us to concentrate on those values. Such concentration helps us find our finer selves, act more responsibly, better control our passions, come to some deeper understanding of a given situation, reach out for a resolution of what troubles us. This is what we mean when we suggest that God is, we do. The purpose of prayer is not to change God, but to change the person praying.

Does God answer prayer? Not really. We do. We find answers to our prayers by concentrating on the best we can think, feel, and then decide to do. Sometimes we call this insight, sometimes inspiration. Some people even call it revelation. They are really all the same. It is our conscious self, concentrating intently on whatever it is that might cause us to turn to God in prayer, which because of the intensity of the concentration brings an "answer" or a sense of relief.

God does not manipulate or change the intimate details of a person's life as an accommodation to that individual's momentary personal needs. But clearly people invoke God, involve their idea of God in their own personal affairs. How can this be best done to avoid despair or disillusionment? How can it be done in ways that are consistent with reasonable expectations of fulfillment?

We have all attended an athletic game at which a member of the clergy or even a layperson led the assembled fans in a prayer for their community's team to win the game. Should God be expected to confer to each side its desired response of victory? Or should we be praying in a different way, or perhaps not at all? It seems to me that the only legitimate prayer that might be uttered before a game is not for victory, but for the health and safety of the players, especially since the possibility of physical harm and injury is inherent in the very nature of the game. I have never heard anyone lead a stadium full of fans in such a prayer. Nor am I aware that fans or relatives of players have ever requested such a prayer. Yet, ironically, I suspect that if a player were seriously injured, his parents and friends would pray fiercely for his recovery.

The fact is that we abuse prayer. The great Christian theologian Reinhold Niebuhr understood its true nature when he composed his "Serenity Prayer," now used in the Twelve Step program of Alcoholics Anonymous. Its simple straightforwardness is a lesson in theological honesty: "God, grant me the serenity to accept the things I cannot change, courage to change the things I can, and wisdom to know the difference."

Although there is no justification for such prayers, in times of war it is common to hear leaders of both sides pray to God to lead their nation's army to victory. As in the simpler, less deadly athletic contests, both sides believe that God is on their side of the struggle. During the First and Second World Wars, German soldiers wore, as part of their uniforms, belt buckles with the inscription *Got mit uns* (God is with us).

For a nation's people not to pray for victory in wartime would be considered almost an act of treason. This may be understandable, but would not a prayer for peace be more appropriate? Creating a "Peace Sabbath," when a nation could focus on ways to achieve peace and resolve to pursue those ways, could shift the nation's attention from devices for killing to techniques for living harmoniously, even with those whose social and political views differ from their own. Perhaps all this seems naive and idealistic on my part. It is certainly hard to imagine Israelis and Palestinians praying together for peace in the Middle East, but eventually they, too, might tire of killing each other and seek ways of reconciliation. They might pray separately at first, and then later some brave soul(s) might bring them together. If it could happen in Northern Ireland, it could happen elsewhere. Is humanity ready for such a change of spiritual and intellectual direction? Pray that it is, for there is simply no alternative if we are to survive.

Mark Twain's famous essay "The War Prayer" subjects the idea of wartime prayer for victory to scathing ridicule. The scene is a church service on a Sunday morning, immediately prior to the mustering of a battalion of fresh troops filled with visions of victory. The pastor blesses them with passionate rhetoric:

> "Bless them, shield them in the day of battle and the hour of peril, bear them in His mighty hand, make them strong and confident, invincible in the bloody onset, help them to crush the foe, grant to them and to their flag and country imperishable honor and glory."

Suddenly, an unkempt and obviously unbidden stranger appears and ascends the pulpit. The preacher concludes, "'Bless our arms, grant us the victory, O Lord our God, Father and Protector of our land and flag!'" Then the stranger says:

> "I come from the Throne — bearing a message from Almighty God! . . . When you have prayed for victory you have prayed for many unmentioned results which follow victory. . . .
>
> ". . . O Lord, our God, help us to tear their soldiers to bloody shreds with our shells; help us to cover their smiling fields with the pale forms of their patriot dead; . . . help us to lay waste their humble homes with a hurricane of fire; help us to wring the hearts of their unoffending widows with unavailing grief; help us to turn them out roofless with little children to wander unfriended the wastes of their desolated land in rags and hunger and thirst, sport of the sun-flames of summer and the icy winds of winter, broken in spirit, worn with travail, imploring Thee for the refuge of the grave and denied it — for our sakes who adore Thee, Lord, blast their hopes, blight their lives, protract their bitter pilgrimage, make heavy their steps, water their way with their tears, stain the white snow with the blood of their wounded feet! We ask it, in the spirit of love, of Him Who is the Source of Love. . . . Amen." . . .
>
> It was believed afterward that the man was a lunatic because there was no sense in what he said.

Twain's bitter cynicism, laced with sarcasm, forces us to look at the issue of a prayer's validity. What would happen if we insisted that prayers for victory be forever banned from our religious institutions and demanded that our religious leaders lead us only in prayers for peace? Imagine a prayer that, instead of asking for victory, urged us to help bring a conflict to an end, to use our talents and the skills of our leaders to effect a permanent and lasting peace rather than to plan another attack — a prayer that would urge generals and politicians immediately to declare a moratorium on slaughter and sit down together to resolve the differences that brought on the fighting.

THE VALIDITY OF PRAYER

The issue of the legitimacy or validity of prayer is intimately connected to the frequently asked question of whether prayers are answered. All who pray would like to believe that their efforts are not in vain, that there is indeed someone or something out there that hears and responds to their pleas, their requests, even their expressions of gratitude. The psalmist tried to reassure us that this is so when he wrote, "God is nigh to all who call upon Him, to all who call upon Him in truth" (Ps. 145:18–19). But I would suggest that some prayers, while seemingly valid, should be rejected. A colleague of mine used to say, "No is also an answer."

Centuries ago, Judaism reached the quite modern conclusion that some prayers are not proper prayers and thus do not deserve to be answered. One of our most respected teachers, Rabbi Nahman of Bratslav, a town in eastern Poland, once said, "Do not ask God to change the laws of nature for you." In other words, prayer should not be used in the hope of inhibiting natural processes. For instance, clerics in a drought-stricken area might ask their congregants to pray for rain, while a thousand miles away, in the midst of a torrential downpour, religious leaders implore their flocks to pray for the rain to end. It is surely not reasonable to expect such prayers to be answered.

We find in the Talmud a warning that a man whose wife is pregnant should not pray for the child to be a boy or a girl. God severely chastised Job for excessive and unacceptable hubris when he begged God to answer his pleas for personal justice: Why should I answer you? In this vast cosmos, who and what are you that I should be mindful of your plea?

> Then the Lord answered Job out of the whirlwind and said:
> Where were you when I laid the foundations of the earth?
> Declare if thou hast the understanding.
>
> . . . .
>
> When the morning stars sang together
> and all the sons of God shouted for joy?
>
> . . . .
>
> Can you bind the chains of the Pleiades
> or loose the bands of Orion?
>
> . . . .
>
> Wilt thou condemn me, that thou may be justified?

Job finally began to understand the enormity of God's selfhood and the smallness of his own suffering, and he responded:

> I have uttered that which I understand not,
>
> . . . .
>
> I heard of Thee by the hearing of the ear,
> but now mine eyes seeth Thee.
> Wherefore I abhor my words, and repent,
> seeing I am dust and ashes.

Job 38:1–42:6

Should I have turned to God in prayer when I first noticed 'Scintillation' dropping leaves and asked God to stop the disease that was consuming my plant? Most would agree that would have been unjustifiable prayer.

The way we use prayer raises many troubling issues. We are frequently disappointed when what we pray for fails to materialize. We expect God to deliver, and when that does not happen, we sometimes become angry or bitter. We begin to doubt God's power. Much of this disappointment is linked to our all-too-human predilection for anthropomorphizing God — that is, ascribing human characteristics to Divinity. For example, we like to think that God is a God of justice, by which we often mean that God makes sure that justice is done. But then we look at the world and see it filled with injustice. We need to stop attributing human qualities to God. God does not do or bring justice to the world. God is an ideal, the representation of perfect justice, which, if we think of it, can inspire us to bring about justice. God, then, is the power that helps us bring justice into the world as we conceive that ideal and work to bring it into our lives. God seen in this way is a power or a force that inspires, not a person who acts on our specific issues. God is. We do. When and if we do things that make for more justice in society, we are bringing God into the world. Praying in a way that makes us conscious of our responsibilities to a world that needs justice can be very helpful to us. It eliminates our having to blame God for our failures or to accuse God of impotence when justice is denied or improperly executed. The burden of making justice work is placed on us, not on Divinity.

Let's take another powerful and popular example: the notion that God is love. Without meaning to sound heretical or impious, let me suggest that God is *not* love. God is a power that makes for love. In the physical world, we see that at work through the affinity of creatures and things. I see it in my garden all the time. I need the praying mantis and the ladybug to rid my garden of certain pests. I need the bees and the hummingbirds to propagate my flowers. That is why I make certain that I have beds of bright red flowers, such as bee balm, or monarda, growing in the summer garden. Does that mean that I think a hummingbird is in love with a monarda plant? Not exactly, but there is a natural affinity between them that I encourage. Although we cannot yet know with utmost certainty, cosmologists are now telling us that there might be a similar pattern in the limitless cosmos: galaxies are attracted to one another. Love on a transcendental scale is not always of the warm and fuzzy kind with which we are familiar.

As we think about the finest, deepest, most enobling and enabling love we can conceive, we associate it with Divinity, the ultimate power that makes for love. We, in our best moments, try to translate that ideal into human relationships. We do not always succeed, but that is our problem, our failure, not God's. Hate, and the hurt it brings, is not a characteristic of Divinity. It is a product of our human failure.

THE POSITIVE VALUE OF PRAYER

Now that we have explored our original questions, how shall we respond to the woman so ready to abandon what little faith she had in God because her husband, Maury, died despite her best, most fervent prayers? A wonderful Talmudic story relates how a distinguished rabbinic scholar lay dying. His disciples gathered around him, praying constantly for the continuation of his life. As long as they prayed, God could not take the rabbi from his life on earth. But the rabbi was old and in pain, and it was time for him to die. His housekeeper, leaning out a window above the courtyard where her patron lay comatose, realized what was happening and decided to intervene in his behalf. She hurled down a clay pot from the windowsill. It smashed on the tile floor, momentarily distracting the disciples from their prayers. In that instant, God snatched up the rabbi's soul.

Somehow I must persuade Maury's wife that she loved Maury as fully and as completely as it is possible for one person to love another and that there comes a point in all our lives when it is time to let go — to let go of life and to let go of trying to forever hold on to life. Our prayers ought to be directed to our own survival in the face of great loss. Our prayers ought to be ones of thanksgiving for years shared with a loved one. Our prayers ought to be expressions of gratitude, not pleas for the unnatural, the impossible.

Not all prayers are requests or petitions. Some of the most beautiful and soul-satisfying prayers are prayers of thanksgiving that bring people peace of mind or a sense of inner well-being. These can have enormous positive value. Prayers in which we associate ourselves with another person in danger, in pain, or in sickness can give comfort to the one for whom the prayer is being uttered. Telling someone "I prayed for you" may be excellent therapy, as it helps the one prayed for feel less isolated, less alone in facing his or her illness. We may dismiss Maury's grieving widow, so angry when her prayers for Maury's recovery went unanswered, but most of us would agree that it was indeed a positive act to pray for Maury. The mistake was that her prayers were misdirected toward his recovery, rather than for the strength to bear the pain she knew his inevitable death would surely bring.

As a rabbi, I have been asked countless times to pray for or with someone. Can anyone deny such a request? Hardly. Nor should we. Joining with another in prayer can be mutually energizing. Moreover, the person can take comfort from the knowledge that there are others who empathize with him or her, share his or her pain, and sincerely wish for his or her recovery. Such knowledge can reinforce the person's will to recover or perhaps help him or her die with dignity. Here we see a classic instance of how prayer can change *people*, not God. That is what prayer is supposed to do.

Does God hear our prayers? I do not know; no one does. But I do know that we are not the first ones to ask such a question. As far back as biblical days, the prophet Habakkuk complained:

How long, O Lord, shall I cry
And Thou will not hear?

Hab. 1:2

Similarly, the psalmist cried out:

I, O Lord, cry to Thee;
In the morning my prayer comes before Thee.
O Lord, why do you cast me off?
Why do you hide your face from me?

Ps. 88:13–14

Perhaps whether God hears our prayers isn't even the right question to ask. Perhaps the real question ought to be, Do *we* hear our prayers, and do they make a difference in our behavior? Prayer may not be able to mend a broken bone or cure cancer, but it can soothe a broken heart and change a life. And it has. God does not need our prayers. We do.

The way I have proposed we look at prayer may imply to some people that I believe prayer is nothing more than auto-suggestion — the self talking to the self. Prayer might be at least that, but it is more, far more than that. Prayer requires that the one who prays direct the prayer toward a worthy object greater than oneself. Neither we nor God can answer our prayers alone. Rabbi Roland Gittelsohn, in his remarkable text on religious thought for young adults, *Wings of the Morning*, compares the answering of prayers to the lighting of an electric lightbulb: "The electricity itself can't turn the light on, nor can we without the electricity. Electricity is a force with which you and I as human beings must cooperate and which we must use if we want the bulb turned on. Similarly, then, God is a force with which we have to cooperate if we want our prayers to be answered." Gittelsohn carries the analogy further. Prayer, he suggests, is "tuning in" to God:

> Just as radio waves are all around me at all times and in every place, so God as the power or force responsible for life is around me all the time. I do not always hear the radio waves around me. I must have a radio set; I must turn it on and tune it in; then the sound waves which were there all the time are converted into a form which I can hear. When I tune in my radio, what actually happens is that I match the frequency of my set to the frequency of the incoming radio waves. In other words, I do not change the radio waves at all; I do something to my own radio equipment which makes it possible for me to hear the waves that were there all the time. In the same way, I am not always conscious of God being around and near me. Prayer is the process whereby I "tune in," so to speak, to God. I match my "frequency" to God's. I make myself aware of the fact that God is there,

and establish direct relationship and communication between God and myself.

The analogy may seem a bit facile, but it does make the point dramatically and simply.

I miss 'Scintillation'. She is in my prayers. By that I mean that I remember her with much fondness, and I am deeply grateful to all the forces of nature that I was privileged to have her in my life to enjoy for the years we were together. But she is gone now, and I confess, I have found another. Love and life allow for that. True, we had an intense affair, and I shall never forget her, but life goes on. 'Phoebe' is also quite beautiful. Her flower is off-white, with a deep purple throat, and she is a profuse bloomer. She will not take the place of 'Scintillation' in my heart; nothing can do that. But 'Phoebe' is happy in my garden, and she brings me much pleasure. Life is like that. Life must come to an end, and prayer, properly understood, can and does satisfy the mind and soul.

CHAPTER IV

On Compost, Death, and Immortality

The One remains, the many change and pass;
Heaven's light forever shines, Earth's shadows fly;
Life, like a dome of many-colored glass,
Stains the white radiance of Eternity . . .

Percy Bysshe Shelley,
"Adonais"

P rayer plays a constant role in many people's lives, but it seems to take on a particular importance in the presence of death. At such moments, it is not uncommon for even the most irreligious among us to participate in services where prayer is central. Even more strange, many of those prayers speak hopefully or faithfully about the prospect of life continuing after death. But does it make any sense to pray for life at a time of death? Where does one begin to find a response to that question? For me, it began in our kitchen.

Garbage has always been plentiful in our home. When the children were young, no matter how much they ate — and our kids were very good eaters — plates and platters frequently left the table half full. There were, of course, leftovers, but somehow, no matter how imaginative my wife was with the remaining food, there always seemed to be a lot of garbage. What to do with it? For years, we did what most people do: we threw it out — at first into a garbage can that was periodically emptied, and later, with the advent of new inventions, into the electric disposal in our sink.

Frankly, I never gave the matter a second thought. That was what one did with garbage. It was only when I began to garden that my postculinary habits changed radically. Garbage, the messier and the more the better, suddenly took on new meaning for me — and new life. In fact, that is exactly what happens to it when it is used in the garden: it takes on new life. Put differently and much more to the point, what seems dead lives — again. Farmers know this about manure. That is why it is saved from the barn and spread over the fields in the spring and fall. Rare indeed is the person who grows things, no matter how inexperienced, but does not know that garbage, like manure, is like brown gold — potential compost, richly alive with the three elements requisite for any successful growing medium: nitrogen, phosphorus, and potash. Nitrogen is vital for the development of leaf and stem growth, phosphorus stimulates strong foliar growth and fruit formation, and potash plays a vital role in the development of chlorophyll and makes plants more resistant to disease.

Through the process of decay, compost, the name we give to seemingly dead plant material that has decomposed, becomes rich in these nutrients. When spread over a garden bed, it becomes the heart and soul of all successful plant life.

No wonder that in the fall, gardeners take their dead leaves and dump them onto the compost pile, usually located, like an old cemetery, in some obscure corner of the yard. No wonder that during the summer, we daily tote our garbage pails to the compost pile and pour the seemingly offensive, potentially foul-smelling waste into a previously dug hole somewhere in the middle of the existing mound. The closer we are to a wild space, the deeper the hole — an attempt to keep the fresh material away from some marauding raccoon. (A useless effort: short of extensive fencing, it is simply impossible to keep a raccoon out of a compost pile. Make the deal: they get half; you get half. Fair is fair.)

During the growing season, we spend serious time at the compost pile, pitchfork in hand, laboriously turning the pile and thus encouraging it to heat up — to increase its physical temperature and thus burn out any undesirable weeds. Lime is also frequently added to a compost pile: first to "sweeten" it — that is, to reduce its acidity — and second to speed the process of deterioration of the plant material. The use of lime for such a purpose has been known and practiced for at least five thousand years. In biblical days, and even before, we know that the dead were placed in limestone caves, called sepulchres. The possession of a family burial cave was critically important, as we have seen in the twenty-third chapter of Genesis, which describes Abraham's desperate bargaining with a local tribe of Hittites, seeking to enlist their help in persuading one of their members, Ephron, son of Zohar, to sell Abraham the cave of Machpelah as a burial site for Sarah, his recently deceased wife. At this juncture in his life, Abraham was a landless sojourner in Canaan, so he needed to procure such a place in which to bury his wife. But the acquisition of even a small plot of ground was more than just a matter of practicality; it was also symbolic. It represented for Abraham, and for subsequent generations, the promise of a future larger settlement on land legitimately acquired through purchase, not conquest. At some later time, these family burial tombs must have become communal.

In Israel, one can visit a very famous cemetery of such sepulchres, carved deep into a huge limestone hill near the ancient Jewish town of Beit Shearim in western Galilee. There, two thousand years ago, our forebears buried their dead in niches, called *kochim*, carved out of the soft limestone. As in the many other burial caves scattered throughout the land, the deceased lay in their shrouds for a year until the lime had eaten everything except their bones. These would be reverently gathered up and put in engraved ossuaries, which were placed in corners of the cave, by then a mausoleum. A visit to Beit Shearim can be an impressive and sobering experience.

Jesus was buried in such a place. Three of the four synoptic Gospels tell us that after his death, he was taken to the Jerusalem burial cave of Joseph of Arimathea, where his body, properly wrapped, was left in a limestone burial niche. What happened after that is the subject of religious belief and considerable theological speculation. Many people believed, and continue to believe, that his life did not end. That is not surprising. People have always been reluctant to accept the idea that death is final. There will always be people who believe passionately that there is conscious life after death and that the living can be in contact with the dead. I find that hard to accept. There are no known, scientifically substantiated cases in which a person who has died has been brought back to speak with the living. Ghost stories are fun; haunted houses are scary; poltergeists are amusing; sessions with Ouija boards can leave one breathless and perplexed. But do any of these phenomena or experiences give any real credibility to the belief that there is conscious life or even some form of physical life after death? You, dear reader, can answer those questions to your own satisfaction. By now you can probably deduce what my response would be to such claims and questions. Nevertheless . . .

As a gardener, I know that renewed or simply new life is not something unusual; it happens annually in my garden. We call it spring. Gardeners revel in spring. Even the original Easter was a celebration of that time, for its origins lie not only in the rites of spring associated with early Germanic tribes but also in the practices of the ancient Persians and Egyptians, who colored and ate eggs at spring festivals. Have you ever wondered why eggs and bunny rabbits are involved in Easter celebrations? Eggs have always been symbols of new life, and rabbits, although they obviously do not lay eggs, are extremely prolific reproducers. Since Easter and its predecessor, Passover, are both in part celebrations of hope for renewal, eggs are featured in their rituals. A roasted egg is part of the Seder plate in the first Passover meal, although interestingly enough the Haggadah, the book that details the order of the Seder meal service, provides no specific blessing to make over the egg. It is just eaten as another appetizer after the general blessing over the food is recited.

Spring is the time when the earth softens and the air turns fresh with the promise of new life. I can smell that moment on the occasion of the first spring visit to my compost pile. Good compost has that fragrance. It is full of life. Literally. I do not know where the worms come from, but turn your pitchfork in a compost pile in spring, and there they are, by the hundreds. Out of the seeming end of living material — in this instance, plant and vegetable matter — life, at least in the form of worms, emerges. Moreover, compost itself seems to contain at least the ingredients for new life, if not indeed new life itself. The more I garden, the more I am impressed with the realization that little, if anything, goes to waste in the natural world. It is a fact that fills me with wonder and wondering.

After all, as a rabbi, I deal with death constantly. I sometimes see people die under the most cruel conditions. I have buried my parents. I have buried one of my children. And I have learned that you never fully recover from putting your own child into a coffin.

A DEATH IN THE FAMILY

It is more than a quarter century since my daughter, Elisa, died accidentally in France. She was only seventeen. She had been on a biking trip there. One afternoon, the group camped near a stable, and Elisa asked if she could go riding. She knew how to ride, and the counselor gave her permission. The stable master, not knowing her level of skill, gave her a gentle horse, and she joined a small group of locals for what was to be an easy trail ride. Elisa had a cold, and she was taking some (too strong) medicine prescribed for her by a French doctor. (We later found the unused portions of that medicine in her pack.) It was a hot, muggy afternoon, and from all accounts of what happened, on the way back to the stable, after being on the trail for an hour, Elisa seemed to lose consciousness and simply fell off the horse. We think that fatigue; the warm, humid weather; and the medication overwhelmed her. She was not wearing a helmet, and her head hit a rock. She died from a subdural hematoma twenty-four hours later in a small French clinic.

How do we as parents face and deal with the death of a child? After all, children are supposed to bury parents, not the other way around. But many parents have experienced such a loss, and none can ever be prepared for the shock. At the time it happened to my family, I discovered some important ways to release my pent-up emotions. Talking about what happened and talking about Elisa helped. And even after more than a quarter of a century, writing about it (again) brings ever-needed consolation.

Elisa's death was an *accident*. I extrapolate nothing of either the demonic or the divine from what happened. I do not believe that God was testing or punishing her mother or me with her death. God is not punitive. That kind of thinking is a cheap replacement for honest thought. Elisa, a firm realist, would have been the first to tell you so.

Neither do I ask why this happened to me, to us. I know why the accident happened. I do not curse God because of it. There is no one to blame for what happened. Elisa was as eager to take the trip on which she died as we were to have her go. We have not been robbed. To the contrary, if one is to speak in those terms, I would say that we were greatly gifted by her presence in our midst, brief as it was.

The measure of our capacity to handle the death of a loved one is, I believe, tested by the way in which we are able to accept the fact, to understand that there is a reality to life that goes beyond time and space. It is called energy — the spirit to which we gain access through memory.

At first, the pain of Elisa's loss engulfed me like a giant wave. Over the years, that wave came with less frequency and less ferocity. Now the sea of my grief is calm, but the pain of my loss has never gone away completely. Nor would I want it to. That would rob me of Elisa's memory. Moreover, I have always had my work to return to. Without that work, without a task unfulfilled that challenges and beckons me, I do not think I could have survived the loss of my daughter. Work — a sense of the as yet unfinished — is crucial to facing grief.

As grieving parents, we were perhaps a bit more fortunate than others, for Elisa was a budding poet and writer, and after she died, we had her writing. Like many adolescents, Elisa was a very private person. As we read through her essays, poetry, and prose observations, a part of the life that death stole from us seemed to be returned to us. From these bits and scraps — some quite adolescent, a few surprisingly mature — we learned much about her that we did not know and might never have known were she still alive. We also had her library. By the end of her short life, it had become a fine reflection of her tastes and interests: Kurt Vonnegut, Dylan Thomas (to whom she introduced me), Isaac Bashevis Singer, Elie Wiesel, Hermann Hesse. After her death, I would go through the books on her shelves and delight in her notes and textual underlining. New doors to her mind would open for me. Sometimes I thought I knew why she had underlined a specific passage; other times I simply wondered why that particular phrase or paragraph hung on a hook in her mind. That, too, restored me.

Death and I are not strangers to each other.

FINDING MEANING
IN THE COMPOST PILE

Does what I learn from my compost pile help me face the realities of my professional and personal life? Indeed. It is in a compost pile that one confronts death and life in stark terms.

For clergy, such confrontation is unavoidable. We are forced to deal with those realities every day. But make no mistake — there is an enormous difference between contemplating the end of a rutabaga gone bad on my porch during a warm spell in February and the death of a friend or family member. I do not mourn the death of the turnip. I deeply mourn the loss of my daughter and others dear to me. I have no lasting memories of the life of a rotten head of lettuce. I am every day reminded of some joyous moment I shared with a loved one.

The compost pile — creating it, nurturing it, turning it, drawing from it — gives me a deeper understanding of life, death, immortality, and new life. Its simple wisdom got me through the trauma of having to bury my closest friend, who, owing to medical incompetence, died on an operating table. It helped me deal with the death of the delightful, charming, beautiful twelve-year-old daughter of one of my congregants, who died of AIDS, a virus inadvertently injected into her at age one in what proved to be a fatal transfusion. My garden's "cemetery" helped me console the young single mom's otherwise unconsolable grief. What could I say when she sobbed out to me, "It's not fair. It's not fair. I'll never see her again. How can God be so cruel?" How does my knowledge of the properties and importance of compost on a garden in the spring help me comfort the father of an eleven-year-old who, at one in the morning, woke him up complaining of a fierce headache and by seven was dead of an aneurysm?

There is more to life than "seeing." There is a dimension to life that we cannot see, touch, feel, smell, or hear. It is caught up and preserved in memory. It survives in our consciousness after another's death. It is regenerative. By drawing on our memory of one physically lost to us, we can continue to renew that person's presence in our lives. As the life in a compost pile is unseen when one merely looks at a pile of rotting material, so is human life incompletely seen or appreciated when one tries to understand it only through the five senses.

Stu Campbell, a smart gardener and a writer, recently published a book called *Let It Rot!* It is a good, readable, complete guide to composting. But it is the title that intrigues me. The title says it all: let it rot. Do not be afraid of death and decay. Do not try to impede the process, which is relentless. There is an intelligent, intelligible, explicable reason behind what happens in a compost pile. We know how decomposition works and why. We know what microorganisms (such as bacteria and fungi) do for and to decaying material. By continually digesting raw material such as grass clippings, garbage, and leaves, microorganisms keep a constant flow of nutrients going to plants. As Campbell tells us, "To grow and multiply, micro-organisms need four things: an energy source, or carbon, a protein source, or nitrogen, oxygen, and moisture." The bulky plant material in the garden is a fine source of carbon. Manure and green vegetation are sources high in nitrogen. Turning a compost pile frequently introduces oxygen, which is required to produce the efficient bacteria called aerobes. These break down the carbon and produce energy, which is why a good compost pile, properly working, gets hot. But beyond all this technical information, we know that whether we do it correctly or not, efficiently or inefficiently, the moment we start a compost pile, we are creating a micro-community, whose population and character will be constantly changing and self-adjusting. We are initiating a series of events and conditions over which we have only minimal control.

Campbell writes, "If you feel somewhat god like as you first create your little universe in your backyard, your growing astonishment at the scope and speed of what is happening will replace whatever feelings of power you may have with real humility." And isn't this exactly what life is like and what it is all about? We create — but oh so quickly, what we create is out of our control. Things happen that we can neither predict nor govern. Our task is not to avoid creating, but to learn how to best use the products of our creative processes and, when necessary, how to let go, to let them die.

It is clearly a lot easier to do this in a garden than in the garden of life. Why is one person cut down in his prime while another lives to old age? Genes? Good self-maintenance? Good medicine, appropriately taken? Luck? All of these are at play, and probably a whole lot more. There is a sound reason for what happens in a compost pile, just as there are sound reasons for why we live as long or as briefly as we do and why we die when we do. The problem is that when death comes before *we* think it should, we are unwilling to accept these reasons. That is our problem, not God's.

All of us carry around horror stories. We all may have reason to curse God and turn away. Some people follow these impulses. I understand that anger, but I think we can do better than just be angry, sullen, or turned off.

It is obvious and tautological to say that death is a part of life. We all know it, but few of us want to accept it. We think that it is going to avoid us, that we can somehow escape it and the pain it inflicts like a dagger wound. We even think we can control the time it will strike. We think we are entitled to at least the biblical threescore and ten years of joyous life for ourselves and those we love. And with the skills of modern science and medicine, we have come to expect even more.

How selfish. If death is a part of life, let us also add that death is neither ugly nor defiling nor a punishment inflicted on those who survive. Death *is*, and without it, there is no life. This is the lesson my humble compost pile teaches me.

There is a wonderful rabbinic story that illustrates this point. A great teacher was dying. One of his disciples turned to God in prayer, begging that the teacher's life be spared. God responded, "Your teacher can live, but understand that so long as he does, so will everything else remain in status quo. There will be no other deaths, no new births, no growth, no decay, no change. Do you want that? The choice is yours. Choose now." The disciple thought for a moment and replied, "No. Life must go on. Take our teacher." At that instant, the rabbi died.

Nor should we fear death. While there is no need to welcome it, except as a release from terrible and irreversible pain, there is also no reason to be afraid of it. The ancient Greeks had it right: when we are, death is not; when death is, we are not; so why fear death? All theories, speculations, "reports from the other side," near-death experiences, and extrasensory perception powers to the contrary, the plain and simple fact is that our only sure knowledge is that after we die, our physical body disintegrates.

Many people do not want to face this obvious reality. I remember when a particularly wonderful family in the congregation lost the mother to cancer. She was only thirty-six years old, and she left not only a grieving husband but also two young children, one a girl about ten. Despite all urging to the contrary, the father and his family refused to have the children attend the funeral, and of course they did not go to the cemetery for the interment. I believed that they were making a serious mistake and told them so. To no avail. Within a week, the father called me. "Charlotte does not believe that her mother is dead," he said. "She never saw her dead, and she insists that her mother is only away and will come back home soon."

Clearly, it was time Charlotte and I sat down to talk. "Charlotte, will you take a small trip with me?" I asked.

"Where to?"

"The cemetery."

Her father was aghast. In all honesty, I was more than a little nervous about what I was planning, but I knew of no other way to deal with the problem. I turned to her father. "Trust me," I pleaded.

Charlotte's curiosity overcame her fear, and she joined me in the car. During the ride, we said little to each other about death. I stopped near the fresh grave, and we walked to it. The fading flower bouquets were still lying on top of the newly mounded soil. We stood by the grave. "Charlotte," I asked, "have you ever seen anything die?"

"Yes. My turtle and my goldfish, and I once found a dead robin in the street."

"What did you do with the goldfish?"

"I flushed it down the toilet."

"What about the turtle and the bird?"

"I buried the turtle in the backyard. I walked away from the bird."

"Why?"

"Because it was all yucky."

"What does 'yucky' mean?"

"You know, rotting. It looked terrible, and it was smelly. I didn't want to get near it."

"Charlotte, that is what happens when things die. They get yucky — only we don't call it that. We say they decompose. A tough word, but what it means is that they go back to being what they originally were before they were born: stuff.

"So why are we here now, talking about all this? Why? Because this is where your mom's physical body is now. Right here, under this mound of soil and flowers. When people die, we bury them in the earth. The earth takes in their bodies, and they become part of the larger physical world. Charlotte, your mom was very sick — so sick she could not survive. She died, and we have done with her what you did with your turtle. We have returned her to the earth."

I need not tell you, dear reader, that tears poured out of my eyes as they poured out of Charlotte's. We both stood there, hugged each other and had a good cry.

"Is she really dead and gone?" Charlotte asked me.

"Dead? Yes. Gone? No. The real part of your mom is inside you. In your memory. Want to tell me about what you most remember about her?" We walked away from the grave site talking about her mother.

That experience confirmed a previous conviction of mine: we cannot and should not hide from death. Since then, I have always encouraged families to have children attend funerals and share in the graveside experience. Death is a reality from which children should not be shielded. They have a right and a need to experience that reality. That, too, is a part of life.

We know what happens *when* we die. We do not know what happens *after* we die. We really do not know. We can *believe* whatever we want to, whatever gives us inner peace, whatever satisfies our inner reason. That is a personal matter. But as for the rest — the speculations, the reports from the other side, the near- and after-death experiences — these are at best highly speculative and at worst deceptive and sometimes cruel in what they lead people to expect.

THE IMPERSONALITY OF DEATH

Death is impersonal. Neither you nor I nor anyone else has the right to think that the Source of Life (some call it God) will or should pay any attention to us when we pray for death to leave our loved ones alone. The great cosmos of which you and I are a part is as impersonal as it is enormous and infinite. It operates under its own system of law and order. It may even have a purpose to its being, although that is highly conjectural. It may be — and I, for one, believe it is — life-affirming. Putting it another way, the cosmos is not in business to put itself out of business. While there is disagreement among cosmologists and astrophysicists, there seems to be a majority view that the cosmos is an expanding, rather than a contracting, phenomenon. Dead things do not expand. (Oh, yes, I know, they bloat for a while, but that is part of the decaying process and is soon over.) Living things expand.

So the cosmos may be "alive," but it is not here to do my or your bidding. The Source of Life is not some personal servant, waiting for you to call in an order for whatever it is you may want at any given moment. It took the great biblical character Job some time to learn that. As I commented earlier, after all of Job's legitimate protestations that he had done no wrong and did not deserve the grief inflicted on him, he turned to God for justice, demanding to know why God either inflicted all those terrible things on him or allowed them to happen. When God finally responded, Job was totally humbled. He and those of his world always thought of themselves as being at the center of things, with the world designed to do their bidding. Never had humans seen themselves as peripheral to the universe. Never had they seen the universe as heliocentric, not homocentric. The writers of the Book of Job turned that perception on its ear.

Then Job answered the Lord:

Behold, I am of small account;
what shall I answer thee?
I lay my hand upon my mouth.
Once have I spoken, but I will not answer again;

.   .   .   .

I know you can do everything.

.   .   .   .

I uttered that which I did not understand,
things too wonderful for me, which I knew not.
I heard of Thee by the hearing of the ear,
but now mine eyes seeth Thee.
Wherefore I abhor my words, and repent,
seeing I am dust and ashes.

Job 40:3—42:6

Job finally began to understand: God did not *owe* him anything. In the great cosmic grinding, Job, like any of us, is just one small, infinitesimal spark. Important, yes, but not so important that God should be concerned with one small, not too critical human: Job or me or you.

The writer of Psalm 8 well understood and beautifully reflects Job's painfully learned humility. I get goose bumps every time I read this magnificent passage:

O Lord, our Lord,
How glorious is Thy name in all the earth!

.   .   .   .

When I behold Thy heavens, the work of Thy fingers,
The moon and the stars, which Thou hast established;
What is man, that Thou art mindful of him?
And the son of man that Thou thinkest of him?

Ps. 8:1—4

The psalmist is not satisfied. Having recognized God's sover-eignty over all, having acknowledged God's enormity, he rhetorically asks, "Is there no room for us? Are we humans totally insignificant in this vast cosmic experiment?" His re-sponse is profoundly reassuring:

> Yet Thou hast made him but little lower than the angels
> And hast crowned him with glory and honor.
> Thou hast made him to have dominion over the works of
>   Thy hands;
> Thou hast put all things under his feet.
>
> . . . .
>
> O Lord, our Lord,
> How glorious is Thy name in all the earth.
>
> *Ps.* 8:5–9

The psalm is breathtaking in its poetic profundity. Job and the psalmist shared the same understanding. Insignificant as we are when seen in the context of cosmic greatness, we humans are not irrelevant or meaningless. We have an important role to play in the evolution of the world's life.

Theologians say all this in a more complex way. They tell us that one of God's attributes is transcendence and that God is above personal concern for the earth and its affairs. That may be all well and good, but when death comes or tragedy strikes, we do not want some abstract philosopher's God out there doing whatever it is that Divinity does in the cosmos. We want a nearby, close God — one we can cry to, one who will mourn with us and empathize with our pain. We want to bring God as close to us as we can, in a most personal way. Thus we seek to make God immanent, near. In all of this, remember, this is what *we* do, not what God does. God is. We do.

As we personalize God in life, so do we personalize

death. We say things such as "Sarah's eternal spirit is now with God." Does such a phrase reflect reality, or is it just poetic rhetoric, recited at funerals to assuage the feelings of pain and loss that the clergy know are persuasive at such a moment?

Scientists tell us that energy can be neither created nor destroyed. Energy is *infinite*. True enough. Not even the most hard-bitten atheist would argue with that statement. Equally true is that our deceased Sarah was (or is?) energy. Now she lies dead before us. What has happened to her energy? If the scientists are right (and we have no reason to suspect what they tell us), Sarah's energy is infinite. Sarah is without end. Cold comfort for people in mourning. At such a time, most of us are not much interested in this kind of descriptive analysis. We want something warmer, some more personal thought, some words that will bring comfort to our broken hearts. We turn to the language of the poets. For *energy*, they might substitute the word *spirit*, and for *infinity*, they might find the word *eternal* more appealing. George Eliot's "The Choir Invisible" is a magnificent example of this poetic softening of language:

> O, may I join the choir invisible
> Of those immortal dead who live again
> In minds made better by their presence; live
> In pulses stirred to generosity,
> In deeds of daring rectitude, in scorn
> Of miserable aims that end with self,
> In thoughts sublime that pierce the night like stars,
> And with their mild persistence urge men's minds
> To vaster issues. . . .
>
> . . . .
> May I reach
> That purest heaven, — be to other souls
> The cup of strength in some great agony,

Enkindle generous ardor, feed pure love,
Beget the smiles that have no cruelty,
Be the sweet presence of a good diffused,
And in diffusion ever more intense!
So shall I join the choir invisible,
Whose music is the gladness of the world.

I have difficulty discerning the difference between energy and spirit. Both words seem to describe something that is not easily determinable by the five senses but that has a definite reality. Similarly, infinity and the eternal seem to suggest the same thought — that which has no end. I find myself asking: In practical, real terms, what is the difference between saying that energy is infinite and that spirit is eternal?

Now, perhaps, the leap of faith that death seems to ask us to take is not so great. To say that Sarah's spirit is eternal no longer seems like some fuzzy religious rhetoric, so much as it sounds like a truth couched in poetic, spiritual, or religious terms. Let us carry the leap of faith one step further: Sarah lives! Sarah is *immortal!*

WHAT IS IMMORTALITY?

Can one really believe in immortality? Yes. At least in what one might call the immortality of great creativity.

Of course, Shakespeare is immortal. But all that means is that his works have outlived him, not that he continues to live after his death in some ill-defined time/space capsule. Besides, there are very few Shakespeares. To create something memorable is a worthy goal, but in fact most of us won't even come close. Our thoughts are droll, our words common, and our actions completely forgettable. The trouble with ordinary people is just that. We are ordinary, too ordinary.

"You look just like your father, may he rest in peace." How many times have we heard or said something like that? As we do, we affirm our belief in genetic immortality. I have my father's nose (too big), and the shape of my thumbs mirrors the shape of his (stubby). There is no arguing with this immortality. We carry the genes of our forebears in our DNA. Our pursuit of immortality begins to warm up a bit. We are getting closer. We want to believe that we survive after death. We can take a modicum of comfort from the knowledge that we are immortal at least through our genetic traces.

There is a beautiful phrase in the prayer book used by Reform Jews during the High Holy Days. At one point in the services, we remember those dead who were lost in war or persecution:

> They lie at rest in nameless graves. Their resting places in far-off forests and lonely fields are lost to the eye of revering kin. Yet they shall not be forgotten. We take them into our hearts and give them place beside the cherished memories of our own loved ones. They now are ours.

We call this social immortality. We are part of the continuum of humanity. We are shaped by all that preceded us, and what we do and are will affect generations to come. We are part of history and find our immortality through it. True, but in fact who cares? We should — and maybe in our finer moments we do — but when death strikes my house, when someone I love has been taken from me, I take little comfort in the knowledge that over the centuries, he or she will become part of the social immortality of the world.

So where does all this leave us? Can one believe in immortality? Yes, at any and every level. Pick the area in which you find most comfort — creative, genetic, social, personal. A belief in some form of continuity after death is neither absurd nor irrational.

We seem to have strayed a long way from the garden, and it is time to return. I need to tell you a true story about a Montauk daisy that defied death. It will lead me into some ideas about resurrection that I would like to share.

CAN WE BELIEVE IN RESURRECTION?

Montauk daisies are huge, tough perennials that grow like weeds. I had a hedge of them in my Shelter Island garden. They bloom in the fall with large, white, daisylike flowers emerging from buds the size of marbles, and they can be quite spectacular. Unfortunately, my hedge rarely made it to bloom. The deer — wise critters that they are — would wait all summer until the buds became fully ripe, and in a night, the buds would disappear, nipped to nothingness by those voracious feeders.

When I left Shelter Island, I dug up a couple of the plants and took them with me for my new garden in the Berkshires. They did not do well there. The climate is two zones colder, and while they grew profusely, they rarely budded. When they did, the buds were small and the flowers sparse. I decided that the Montauks were taking up too much room and it was time to get rid of them. One fall, I quite unceremoniously, hastily, and roughly dug out a huge clump and dumped them in the compost pile. *Good riddance,* I thought, and promptly struck Montauk daisies from my list of garden plants and forgot about them. Little did I know.

The next spring, while I was mucking about in the pile, I noticed some small white shoots sprouting through. What in the world? Maybe I had a treasure here I didn't know about. Slowly, I cleared away the covering of mulch. There, springing out of the pile, back in full life, was my Montauk daisy. It had finished its good winter's sleep and was ready again to share its wealth with me. Mirabile dictu. Can dead things live again? I asked myself. Maybe there is some reason to believe in resurrection, a belief I otherwise totally reject.

The compost pile can be as deceptive as it is beguiling. Clearly, I had only mulched the Montauk, when in fact I had intended to compost it. There is a difference between the two. Composting is the name we give to manufacturing new soil. Mulching is the process by which we cover plant material with compost. When we mulch, the primary goal is to reduce weeds and evaporation of moisture from the soil by laying something on the ground. Composting involves mixing organic materials with the soil itself. I had meant to destroy the Montauk. Instead I must have only covered it with a blanket for the winter. That plant was no more dead than seeds left in a packet over the winter are dead.

CHRISTIANITY AND JUDAISM ON RESURRECTION

Christianity affirms that Jesus was resurrected after his death. This belief is one of the chief factors distinguishing Christianity from Judaism. Belief in physical resurrection is precisely that — a belief. But resurrection, as an event, defies anything anyone besides Jesus has ever experienced. Still, millions seem to want to believe in it as a real possibility.

The concept of resurrection is not found in the Hebrew

Bible. It is a postbiblical idea originating with a Jewish sect known as the Pharisees, who began to flourish in the first century before the Common Era (B.C.E. — before the birth of Christ). Some people, however, incorrectly turn to the thirty-seventh chapter of Ezekiel's famous "valley of the dry bones" image as proof that resurrection is a biblical theme. Ezekiel was a prophet of the Babylonian exile whose message anticipated a national restoration in Israel of the people and their kingdom: "Thus says the Lord . . . and I will bring you home into the land of Israel" (Ezek. 37:12). But this was not the prediction of some supernatural event. The Book of Daniel is also frequently cited as confirmation that the Bible contains strong references to resurrection (see Dan. 12:2–3). A late biblical book, written around the second century B.C.E., Daniel was heavily influenced by the eschatological thinking of a Judaism under the boot of Greco-Roman oppression. Its references to an afterlife are not descriptive of mainstream biblical thinking. During this time, the Jewish community gave up hope of achieving national independence and turned their thoughts instead to a better tomorrow.

The intense severity of Roman rule left the Jewish community in Palestine without power and without realistic hope for the restoration of their former glory as a nation-state. As a result of this political despair, irrational hope in a supernatural "redeemer" (which is what the Hebrew word *messiah* means), who would miraculously appear and redeem the people from their misery, began to take hold. The Jewish community started to look forward to that event the same way a gardener in the dead of winter looks forward to spring and its promise of new life. Not only would this messiah save them in the here and now; he would also restore to life even those who had died innocently under the Roman lash.

Thus a concept of resurrection began to grow in Jewish thought. For Jews of that period, it was only a normal extension of a long-held belief that while death marked one's physical end, the human spirit had a continuity as part of the divine economy. As God does not waste anything — the lessons from my compost pile are inescapable — so does God conserve the human spirit. Resurrection remained an accepted concept in Judaism for two thousand years, during centuries that saw Jews hounded by forces shaped by insensitive theologies and brutal politics. Orthodox Judaism still clings to a belief in resurrection, tied to the future coming of the messiah, who will redeem the entire world. But it is not a major leitmotif in Jewish thought. Rather, the emphasis is placed on human endeavor to bring about a messianic age — a time when humans will have so affected the social condition as to achieve peace and justice. In other words, in Judaism, the messianic moment is within our power, not God's. A beautiful rabbinic story illustrates this point. It is said that if you are in the act of planting a tree and someone says, "The messiah is coming, the messiah is coming," you should first finish planting the tree and then go greet the messiah.

The idea of resurrection was well suited to and better served early Christianity. Because it justified Jesus' death, it quickly became incorporated into the literature and theology of the New Testament. Paul made it an essential part of his credo for those he called Christians. By the third century of the Christian era, it became the centerpiece of Christian theology and philosophy.

The early Hebraic ideas of death are utterly amazing when one realizes that the two great civilizations that surrounded ancient Israel, and from which that culture drew so much else, heavily relied on life-after-death beliefs. The

popular belief in Babylon was that the dead moved to the next
world. Excavated Babylonian tombs filled with items to make
that transition comfortable reflect that belief. In Egypt, the
idea was raised to an official level. The realm of death was the
realm of the gods, and human dead could, under certain circumstances, enter that realm. One need go no further than a
visit to a museum containing a display of Egyptian artifacts to
see just how refined became Egyptian belief in the realm of
the dead. The pyramids still stand as brilliant testimony to the
commitment to that ancient Egyptian belief. But something in
the religion of ancient Israel did not allow the Jews to accept
the belief systems of their neighbors. The more Egyptian culture identified life after death with a realm of the gods, the
more biblical Judaism disavowed the idea, making the realm
of the dead impure and corpses contaminating. Judaism did
not see any holiness in death. Death was seen as an end, not a
transition to some other place:

> Whither shall I go from your spirit
> or whither shall I flee from your presence?
> If I ascend to heaven you are there
> If I make my bed in sheol, there will I find you.
>
> *Ps. 139:7−8*

The biblical Sheol is a nebulous region with no judgment, no
reward, and no punishment. The dominant biblical belief concerning death was that a person's individuality was absorbed
back into God.

   This understanding of what happens after death met the
intellectual and spiritual needs of a small but growing liberal
movement within Judaism. It was called Reform Judaism, and
it arose first in Germany in the middle of the nineteenth

century and subsequently prospered in America. These early German reformers, strongly influenced by middle Europe's nineteenth-century currents of political emancipation and its atmosphere of intellectual enlightenment emphasizing rationalism, drew on the Hebrew Bible to completely disavow any belief in resurrection. Instead, they emphasized the idea of spiritual immortality: "Then shall the dust return to the earth as it was. And the spirit to God who gave it" (Eccles. 12:7). Understandably, they evoked the militant ire of Europe's Orthodox Jewish community. Reform Judaism all but died out in Europe, but it has become the largest denomination in American Jewish religious life, embracing some 1,800,000 men, women, and children.

At every graveside service, after the coffin is lowered into the ground, and as I throw shovelfuls of earth on the casket, I recite that passage from Ecclesiastes, and I think of my garden — lying inert under a blanket of snow, with the rain pelting down on it, or in the full sun of summer bloom — and I know. I know that without the dead plant material piled on my compost heap, my garden would not make it. I know too that we all must die, that without death there is no life. And I know that there is more to death than dying. While I do not accept the notion of resurrection, I know that we live on immortally, not in the form that once identified us, but we do live on. It is part of the divine economy inherent in all things. God does not waste a life, any more than nature wastes its detritus. I know this, and I am at peace.

CHAPTER V

Garden-Variety Miracles

Nature and Nature's laws lay hid in night:
God said, Let Newton be! and all was light.

Alexander Pope, Epitaph
intended for Sir Isaac Newton

T he bulb and flower catalogs begin arriving in late January and continue through February. Coming as they do during the peak of winter's drear, they are impossibly beguiling — the drama of the flowers' colors is captivating. The tulip bulbs are usually featured in the front of the catalogs, and one flower is more alluring than the next: the Darwins, the Emperors, the Parrots.

I skip those pages. In fact, I avoid planting tulips for two very good reasons. First, I am lazy. I know that if, after the third year, I don't dig up, divide, and replant the bulbs, they will shrink and eventually disappear. The catalogs don't tell you that when they seduce you with their splendid offerings, but most gardeners know this secret truth about tulips. Second, tulips are favorite appetizers for deer, which wait for the flower heads to almost break into bloom and then attack voraciously. The larger, the more exotic, the more colorful the tulip, the greater the feasting. Deer are not sweet little Bambis. They are gluttonous eating machines that can strip a garden in a night and break a gardener's heart. Their appalling habits can make a grown man cry. As far as I am concerned, be it politically correct or not, deer are terrible pests, and the only way I like them is roasted and served on a plate.

Thank the good Lord that for whatever reason, deer do not like crocuses or daffodils. One can never plant enough of these wonderful flowering bulbs, and I plant lots of both. There is nothing more exciting than seeing the earliest crocuses, with their bright purples, lavenders, and yellows, popping up as the first harbingers of spring. Sometimes they even dare to thrust their small, audacious, perky heads up through the snow as early as late March or the beginning of April.

Daffodils, of course, come a bit later, but they also begin to appear when most of us are still putting on our winter coats before going outside. Each year, I add to my plantings of crocuses and daffodils. Their colors are as gratifying as any tulip bed I have seen, and they never need to be dug and divided. To the contrary. Leave them alone, and certain varieties, once planted, will multiply (a process known as naturalizing) into eye-filling drifts. This profusion of flowers inspired William Wordsworth to write a poem that evokes them perfectly:

I wandered lonely as a cloud
That floats on high o'er vales and hills,
When all at once I saw a crowd, —

A host of golden daffodils
Beside the lake, beneath the trees,
Fluttering and dancing in the breeze.

In springtime, I often think of these lines and remind myself that no gardener, amateur or professional, planted or re-planted that "host of golden daffodils." They just got that way on their own. All of us who do any gardening at all strive each year to develop just such a crowd of daffodils somewhere, everywhere, on our property.

Contrary to popular opinion, daffs are not necessarily yellow. In fact, now that my garden is established, I add only varieties of white. I am particularly addicted to the double-flowering fragrant ones: 'Erlicheer' is a special favorite, as are 'Cheerfulness', 'Sir Winston Churchill', and 'Thalia'. 'Replete', a double-flowering variety, has a splash of color deep in its throat. Many, such as 'Ice Follies' and 'Rosy Cloud', are deeply touched with orange or pink.

Since spring-flowering bulbs are planted only in the fall, they arrive in September and October with printed instructions urging gardeners not to delay in getting them in the ground. The diligent, well-organized gardener plants them as soon as they arrive, while the weather is warm and the bulbs have time to set (develop root systems before frost). The rest of us usually throw them into the shed, promising ourselves to get to the planting ASAP.

But in the fall, there is always too much other stuff demanding our attention. November starts to turn raw. True, you can plant bulbs until the ground has frozen, but digging a couple of hundred six-inch holes — or, for that matter, dig-ging a six-inch-deep bed — for bulbs when it's cold enough that your nose drips constantly on your sweater or parka isn't the most pleasant gardening I know. Each year, I resolve, *Next year, I will do this earlier.* (I never do.)

It's cold, and I'm in a hurry, but there is still time, and I cannot help contemplating these wrinkled, dead-looking things that have arrived in their marked paper bags. Daffodil bulbs are not smooth or sleek like tulip bulbs. Anything but. Frankly, they are kind of ugly, and in any other circumstances, I might be inclined to just toss them away. Take an iris rhizome — the deadest-looking thing I can think of short of a corpse. The leaf stalks — what is left of them — are mostly brown, with only a little green down near the base. The roots are nothing more than stringy tentacles emerging down the side of the elongated, fleshy rhizomes. You plant them on a mound, close to the surface, covered with just enough soil (you hope) to keep the spring thaw from heaving them right out of the ground.

I look at these "dead" things and think, *These will produce flowers next spring?* They do, and the colors that emerge are exactly like the ones pictured in the catalog. It's a miracle. And I don't even believe in miracles. In fact, as a religious liberal, I have always rejected the idea of miracles, considering that miracles and religious belief are a contradiction in terms. And yet those unsightly bulbs do produce the most glorious flowers every spring, without fail.

DO SUCH MIRACLES PROVE GOD'S EXISTENCE?

I can guess what you are thinking at this point. How can a rabbi harbor and, worse, express such thoughts and still parade as a man of faith? Isn't the literature of every religion filled with miracle stories — from Moses' parting of the Red Sea and Joshua's causing the walls of Jericho to fall, to the disappearance of Jesus from his sealed tomb, to Muhammad's miraculous ascent into heaven from the rock in Jerusalem where the famous Mosque of Omar is now built? Doesn't religion teach us to believe in miracles as one of the most potent proofs of God's existence? The answer, of course, is yes to both questions. But I maintain that this approach has done a great disservice both to those who want to believe and to religion itself.

Miracles are presented to us in order to prove the existence of God. Yet on closer examination, it may be that they make belief in Divinity more difficult, if not almost impossible. Most of us come to believe in God by seeing or being taught to understand an astonishing lawfulness in the order of the universe. We use that to justify our belief in and acceptance of God as the source of such order. But since miracles interrupt lawful procedures, does not suggesting that they prove or demonstrate God's existence leave us with an incredible, if not unacceptable, contradiction? I think so.

Theologians have long struggled with this conundrum. Maimonides (1135–1204), Judaism's most famous medieval philosopher and the physician to the vizier of Egypt, rejected miracles and the existence of angels (mentioned frequently in the Bible), just as he opposed magic and superstitious beliefs. Another respected rabbinic thinker, Levi ben Gershon (1288–1344), was explicit in his rationalization of biblical miracles, holding that they never happened as portrayed in biblical texts and explaining them, whenever possible, in a naturalistic way. He wrote that the sun did not really stop for Joshua at Gibeon, but only appeared to do so because Joshua was successful in bringing the battle to a swift conclusion.

But not all Jewish thinkers were or are rationalists. Orthodox Jews have great difficulty dealing with the challenges to their belief that God wrote the entire Hebrew Bible and handed it to Moses on Mount Sinai. Since they believe this, it follows that they accept as true the miracles described in the Bible. Orthodox Jews (and fundamentalist Christians) tend simply to ignore the entire question of biblical criticism.

Most modern Jewish thinkers accept that religious truth and reason are compatible. "Only the simple believeth every word" (Prov. 14:15) is also a maxim of the Jewish faith. The beloved Hasidic master Nahman of Bratslav (1772–1810) went so far as to argue that it is entirely proper that objections can be found to God. But he then turned the argument to his own purpose: "It is right and suitable that this should be so because of God's greatness and exaltedness. Since in His exaltedness He is so far above our minds there are bound to be objections to Him." And today the Orthodox rabbi Louis Jacobs, who practices and teaches in London and is somewhat of an anomaly among his colleagues, is not afraid to tackle the matter of miracles in religion. He uses the festival of Chanukah as a case in point.

Chanukah is one of Judaism's most popular holidays, made more so by the coincidental fact that it occurs annually around the same time as Christmas and also features gift giving. Like Christmas, it has a miracle element woven deeply in its core. The holiday celebrates the triumph of the Maccabees over a Syrian army occupying Palestine circa 165 B.C.E. As the story goes, the Maccabees entered the defiled temple in Jerusalem to rekindle the light over the holy of holies and rededicate the sacred space. They needed sanctified oil for the lamp before the ark, but a search of the premises turned up enough oil for only one day's burning.

Miraculously, though, the oil burned for eight days, giving them time to make and bless a new supply.

Did the miracle of the oil really take place, or is it a legend? According to Rabbi Jacobs, in his 1999 book *Beyond Reasonable Doubt*:

> There is much evidence that the kindling of the lights on Chanukah precedes by centuries the story of the miracle and the oil, and the connection of this with the pagan kindling of lights at the time of the winter solstice has often been noted. Chanukah, and the stress on the miracle of the old, is a creation of the Jewish people. But this creativity has inspired Jews to keep alive the flame of Judaism, and that is the best reason there can be for Jews to continue to celebrate this festival.

In my view, the distinguished Rabbi Robert Gordis had the right idea when he wrote, "The modern religious spirit finds God revealed far more impressively in the majestic harmony and order of the universe than in the miracles which earlier generations delighted to chronicle." I agree. The annual successive outcropping of spring bulbs in my garden — scillas, crocuses, windflowers, daffodils — testifies to Rabbi Gordis's sage observation.

Those who advocate accepting miracles as confirmation of religious "truth" seem to want us to do in the sphere of religion what we would not do in any other aspect of our lives: suspend our critical faculties and accept on faith what defies reason and logic. We would not walk across a bridge built by someone who ignored the laws of mathematics. Neither would we accept any medical diagnosis offered just on faith. Why, then, should we establish our religious commitment based on ideas and beliefs that defy all knowledge, all reason, any proof? Why shouldn't religion be subject to the same canons of logic that we demand of all other forms of critical thinking? In my view, if God is to be understood at all, it is in and through both cosmic and natural law and order, not through their suspension. Miracles contradict the logic of nature and the universe. They reduce our awareness of God to incomprehensibility. Those who use miracles to prove God's existence pinion their beliefs on the inexplicable. We do not do that with any other discipline in our lives. Why should we do it with religion?

The fact is, the belief in miracles, rather than proving the existence of God, asks not only that we suspend our use of reason — the one way we have of understanding God's existence — but also that we trivialize God. God becomes a miracle worker, a magician, some kind of wizard.

I am neither insensitive to nor unaware of the fact that people "find" God in many ways. I love to visit those galleries of the Metropolitan Museum of Art devoted to the Impressionists, where I am reduced to awed silence as I contemplate the genius, the inspiration of a Manet, a Monet, a Soutine, or a Rodin. Their talents could surely be thought of as God given. Similarly, when I listen to Mozart, Brahms, Bach, Beethoven, or Copland, I wonder about the source of their magnificent works. What is the origin of such prodigious genius?

There is no denying that one can find God in great art and music. It is through our most powerful emotions that we may feel closest to God. But finding or feeling close to God and having one's emotions powerfully moved by an event are subjective experiences. We still need to search for objective confirmation of the existence of a power greater than ourselves operating in the world and in the larger universe. That requires bringing to bear all the knowledge science can provide and integrating that knowledge with the most rational thinking that trained intelligence can offer. Otherwise, anyone's belief, regardless of how ill conceived it might be, would be as good as that of some of our world's greatest minds. Were that the case, why would anyone consider learning anything?

UNDERSTANDING GOD THROUGH THE ORDER OF THE UNIVERSE

As I have already suggested, the most persuasive argument I know for believing in a transcendental force — the one we like to call God or Divinity or *élan vital* or by many other names — is this: look at the natural world, look at the universe and its orbiting stars and planets, observe the great cosmos with its ever-dying, ever-expanding galaxies, and see how lawful and orderly things seem to be. Some people argue that there is no guarantee that such a steady state will last eternally. They may be right. We cannot know if it will. But this we do know. It has lasted for the past four billion years, during which men and women have built pyramids, linked otherwise separated seas, erected skyscrapers, sent men to the moon, and built habitable space stations.

Humanity has also misused its great intellectual skills. It is difficult to understand how people capable of such great creativity could use thermonuclear power to destroy Hiroshima and Nagasaki and their vast populations or use conventional weapons to incinerate Dresden during the Second World War. How could political and military leaders intellectually justify such mass destruction? But these horrible brutalities do not challenge the thesis of the existence of some cosmic mind. They reveal the depths to which people can sink when they ignore the lessons the heavens and nature have to teach us. Not even cosmic chaos, which some scientists say is at the heart of the universe, is as cruel as humans seem capable of being. In fact, chaos is not cruel at all. It has or follows its own universal laws. A snowflake obeys mathematical laws with surprising subtlety, and surely a snowflake is not cruel.

The fact remains that the cosmos is extraordinary. And its awesome realities lend great credence to placing long-range trust in the constancy of our discovered laws of physics, mathematics, astrophysics, electricity, and gravity. Throw a stone in the air, and it will always fall at the rate of 32 g, never at any other speed; that gravitational speed remains constant on earth and, from what we can discern, in space as well. If it didn't, the world would fly apart. The laws of thermodynamics are constant. We live in a universe that is orderly and whose laws are dependable. Human behavior may not be, but physical laws seem to be. Each planet and star operates on a strict timetable. Astronomers can predict with pinpoint accuracy where any of the known ones will be at any given time. To an astronomer, the most remarkable thing about the universe is not its immense size, its great age, or even the violence of the forces operating within its borders. The orderliness of the universe is considered to be the supreme discovery of science.

The greatest "miracle" is that human intelligence has rolled back the blanket of ignorance that for so many centuries covered this knowledge. One has to respect that enormous feat. Admittedly, the relationship between science and religion has always been an uneasy, sometimes belligerent, one. The challenge of modernity, however, is no longer to claim superiority of one over the other, to choose one over the other, but to recognize the proper sphere of each and their interpenetration of each as refracted through human thought and human need. (I will deal more deeply with this postmodern situation in chapter 6.)

What is true of the cosmos is true of the natural world. The tides can be timed exactly, which makes an enormous difference to anyone who has anything to do with oceans and seas. A similar regularity may be observed in the growth of seeds. Zinnia seeds always produce zinnias, never bellflowers. Commercial growers and private gardeners know exactly when to start their growing seasons. The union of a human egg with a human sperm will always produce a human, never anything else. Granted, sometimes the product is flawed, but it is never of another genus. We were able to land a man on the moon because we discovered the laws by which the planets operate, calculated accordingly, and hooked up two separately orbiting objects, man and moon. What is even more "miraculous" is that they did indeed come together, way out there in space, exactly as planned. The mathematics worked perfectly, thank God. Best of all, we can repeat that process anytime we wish. Those laws are constant and unchanging. Discovering and then applying them correctly not only enabled us to put men on the moon but also allowed us to send into space, and keep in space, the space stations and satellites that have changed the way we live and think.

Our universe is an orderly place, and that makes all the difference. This fact (and it *is* a fact) even makes people begin to think more seriously and more favorably about the possibility of what some call the Cosmic Mind. Scientists have thought and written extensively about the orderliness of the greater world as one way — maybe the most compelling way — to posit the existence of Divinity. All recognize some organizing force that drives the cosmos and gives structure to evolutionary change.

It is one thing to discover and understand the orderliness of this world and the larger cosmos of which it is a part. That is in and of itself awesome: it fills one with awe and respectful humility when contemplating the vastness of space and time. But it is quite another matter to infer some purpose to that orderliness. Does the universe function in some integrated way toward some end to accomplish some identifiable goal, as does, say, an engine?

ORDER AND PURPOSE

We are now treading on an area that can be intellectually and spiritually dangerous if only because it is so beguiling. We *want* to believe many things that we may not logically be entitled to believe. That will to believe is very strong in most of us. Let us then proceed with great caution.

Order may indeed reflect a purpose. Nature is full of examples in which the purpose is instinctive. It takes place without any conscious intervention on the part of the living plant or animal. Protective coloration is a good example, as are the growth patterns of seeds and plants. If the seed of a plant or tree is put in the ground upside down, the root will reverse itself to grow downward, and the stem will curl around to grow upward. I first learned about this after I planted begonia and caladium tubers upside down. It's easy to make that mistake, and it takes a bit of experience to distinguish top from bottom on these little tubers. The point is that they came up anyway — a bit late that season, but they did appear and flower.

One can see a purpose in the relationship between plant and animal life. It is called symbiosis. Plants need carbon dioxide to survive; animals need oxygen. Plants give off oxygen for animal consumption, while animals exhale carbon dioxide for the nourishment of plants. Neither could long endure without the other. Excessive destruction of plant life, as in the clear-cutting of large areas of trees, eventually puts animal and human life at risk.

Remarkably, bees in flight can take their bearings from the sun even when the sky is overcast, thus keeping their desired direction. Bats have a kind of sonar that keeps them from bumping into objects when they are in flight.

I have gray squirrels in the garden. They raise hell with my bird feeders, but they are intriguing nonetheless. They will store their nuts in six or seven different caches during the autumn. And when winter comes, they find their storage bins, even in the snow. Sometimes, though, they may forget where all their bins are. I have seen oak seedlings sprout from such forgotten storage bins. Woods can be started this way.

Sometimes we turn natural order to human purpose. A peanut contains chemical properties that can be discerned, isolated, and cataloged. It took George Washington Carver to give the peanut's existence and subsequent cultivation a serious purpose and enormous economic meaning. Through research and experimentation, he discovered more than a hundred commercial uses for peanuts and their oil.

Move now back to the vast and mysterious cosmos. As already noted, a growing number of scientists, observing the orderliness of the cosmos, suggest that there is some purpose, some meaning in that. Here we enter the realm of belief, which carries the discussion to another level. I may personally believe that this is as much a purposeful world as it is an orderly one, but when I make such an assertion, I recognize that I am imposing my will to believe on what is demonstrably only orderly.

Before the rise of modern science, people tended to attribute unusual events to some divine intervention, which they often called miraculous. That was understandable, if mistaken. There is a vast difference between standing in awe of the seemingly inexplicable and confusing it with the miraculous. There is no longer any need to identify the as yet unexplained as miraculous, but this does not make our world and the cosmos less awe inspiring. Knowing what we know should only increase our sense of wonder.

If all this does not lead to an irrefutable argument for a purposeful world, at least it shows how extremely plausible is the traditional belief that the glory of God fills all space. Observing the lawfulness of the natural world and the greater universe is really the most credible and, logically, the only way we have to understand the existence of a God force. Law and order is God's essential nature. The psalmist surely had it right when he sang, "The heavens declare the glory of God" (Ps. 19:1).

THE ORIGINS OF MIRACLE TALES

Would it be cruel or unfair to suggest that organized religion seems more concerned with propounding and defending miracles than it is with projecting a religious belief grounded in hard, rational thought? Religionists especially want us to believe in *their* miracles. While each faith may recognize and tolerate the miracle tales of other faiths, each has its own favorites on which it seems to secure much of its particular theology. Christians love the miracles associated with the birth and death of Jesus. Jews celebrate the miraculous legends of the first eleven chapters of the Book of Genesis, as well as those connected with their forebears' exodus from Egypt. Hindus revere the miracle tales surrounding Brahma, Krishna, and Vishnu.

By the same token, though, most religious authorities seem to get very nervous when so-called outsiders or unauthorized personnel introduce miracles of their own. At least once a year, we read or hear of someone, somewhere in the world, who allegedly has experienced a religious miracle. A saint or even the Virgin Mary appears in the person's backyard; word leaks out, and hundreds of the faithful and the curious show up to view this miracle. Then thousands begin to arrive. The church gets nervous, and its spokesperson begins to dissemble: "Yes, of course miracles are possible, but . . . in this case . . . well . . ." Providentially, the sighting eventually fades away. The crowds stop coming. The person who experienced the miracle miraculously becomes silent. The media lose interest and go on to other new sensations. The church breathes a sigh of relief as the matter dies.

Isn't it interesting that so many of these sightings occur in impoverished areas? One rarely associates miraculous occurrences with places of wealth or with people of higher education. Iris Guinazu, an anthropologist who specializes in Argentine folklore, captured the appeal of miracles for many when she observed, in her August 10, 1996, *New York Times* article, "Miracle Child and Answered Prayers": "For these people, Christianity is too much of an abstraction. They believe in what they see or touch. These rites help them to identify with their true selves."

We need to distinguish between miracles and miracle tales. Both have an enormously powerful appeal, and people seem reluctant to give up belief in them. While reports of miracles are usually associated with immediate events, usually experienced only by the person reporting them, most miracle tales seem to evolve from natural phenomena that cannot be explained: a storm laced with thunder and lightning resulting in a forest fire, the appearance of a rainbow, a devastating rainstorm turned into a flood. To those experiencing such frightening events, someone or something must be responsible. Not surprisingly, stories develop to explain what happened — the more powerful and the more fantastic the better. One can see how embellishment may follow; as the story passes from generation to generation, the fantastic can easily turn into the miraculous. Belief may replace reason as a vehicle for acceptance, and the miracle story assumes sacred proportion and status.

The story of the exodus from Egypt, a tale deeply rooted in the Jewish psyche, exemplifies how this can happen. The alleged crossing of the Red Sea by the Hebrew slaves escaping the Egyptian pharaoh and his troops is surely one of the greatest miracle tales ever told. But it probably never happened. The Red Sea back in 1290 B.C.E. was actually a swampy area filled with papyrus, the plant from which Egyptians made paper. In the Bible, it is called the Sea of Reeds (Yam Suf in Hebrew), not the Red Sea (Adom), and it remained a swamp until a Frenchman named Ferdinand de Lesseps initiated construction of the Suez Canal in the late nineteenth century. Such a swamp would hardly be the place for chariots and horses, the tanks of ancient Egypt.

Without my going too deeply into a lesson in biblical history and archaeology, suffice it to say that the Egyptian army probably never pursued the fleeing Hebrews into that swampy area. But for those who later wrote down this story as a focal point in the Jews' sacred history, such a lackluster departure from Egypt could never be a sufficient description of what happened. They were not just writing history; they were writing theology, using history as a base. Every event had to be more than just an event. It had to show that God operated in and through history. The escape of the Hebrews from Egypt had to be seen not just as a natural event, but as one directed by God. Thus their departure became a flight to freedom led by a God of freedom. It had to be seen as a mighty deliverance by a power greater than the pharaoh, the greatest power of that period. It had to be seen as a triumph of the God of gods over the Egyptian gods, the chief of whom was the pharaoh himself. Thus was the exodus embellished, expanded, magnified, and glorified. It had to be seen as a miracle, and indeed it was.

Hollywood and Charlton Heston indelibly fixed that miracle in our minds when they brought the biblical account to the movie screen. Once the parting of the Red Sea became visual, it became irrefutable. That, of course, is the stuff of which miracles are made.

Perhaps at this point you think me a heartless rationalist, devoid of even a shred of emotional warmth or imagination. After all, I have just deconstructed the story of the exodus, one of my people's most cherished tales, the one on which we build the holiday of Passover and its attendant Seder celebration. But miracles do happen, you say. Look at the cures that people who visit the shrine of Lourdes testify to. What about those? And you call yourself a man of the cloth. Shame! Besides, you cannot take away my faith.

THE MIRACLES I BELIEVE IN

What shall I say? I do believe in miracles, just not the kind commonly associated with the Bible. I have seen how strong belief has worked miracles in people's psyches. I know there is a mind-body connection. A colleague and professor, Rabbi Burton Visotzky, profoundly observed, in Winifred Gallagher's *Working on God*, "A miracle is not God, but that which calls your attention to God, as pyrotechnics do. You have to stop, look — pay attention before you hear God's voice." He put it very well.

I remember the day the daughter of one of my congregants called to ask me to visit her father in the hospital. "Dad's in a coma," she said, "but it would mean a lot to us if you would sit with him for a moment. The doctor doesn't have much hope and tells us we do not have a lot more time with him."

That afternoon, I entered his room. Phil and I had known each other for some years. His was not an unusual story except for two facts: he had lived through Hitler's hell, and he loved to sing. I first met him when I was asked to speak to a meeting of Holocaust survivors. We liked each other, and from time to time, he would drop by the synagogue to schmooze. He knew that I had a terrible singing voice but I liked folk music. He taught me three or four Yiddish songs, which on occasion we would sing together when the mood was right.

I sat next to Phil's bed, took his hand, and started to talk to him. No response. I heard his roommate tell me that it was a waste of time. He had been that way for the past ten days. I turned back to Phil and began to hum one of the Yiddish melodies he had taught me. Then, softly, I began to sing another one I had learned from Phil. I sang mostly to myself, I guess. I didn't even know I was crying till the salt ran into the corner of my mouth. I pushed back my chair, let go of Phil, said a silent prayer for him, and left. It all seemed so inadequate. So futile. So stupid, singing to a man who could not hear.

Two days later, I went back to visit Phil. The bed was empty. I turned to his roommate and asked, "Did he die? When?"

"No, Rabbi. He didn't die. He's down in X-ray. That afternoon after you left, he sat up in bed and said, 'Rabbi!' The nurse happened to come by and nearly fainted dead away. He's been awake and talking ever since. I guess he did hear you. They say he's going to make it."

Maybe a miracle? If it was, then I believe in miracles — the miracle of the human spirit. I believe in that. I have also seen the Sistine Chapel in Rome, another miracle of the human spirit, and I know how Michelangelo lay on his back on a scaffold under that ceiling for four torturous years painting ten thousand feet of fresco, finally producing what is possibly the most magnificent and inspiring piece of religious art in history. Michelangelo was a miracle.

I believe in miracles. I believe in the miracle of the orderly universe we inhabit and in our capacity to discern that order. I believe in the miraculous beauty of the shrubbery and trees that surround my garden when the autumn turns their leaves to red and gold and flaming orange. I believe in the miracle of the human body, more complicated by far than the most ingenious piece of machinery invented by humans. And I believe in the miracles of medicine, which every day unravel those mysteries and enable us to cure, heal, and prolong life. I believe in the miracle of bulbs, which, when we plant them properly, will in their time emerge, true to the promised color, form, and fragrance. I believe because I am a gardener.

As a gardener, I believe in the miracles of the peony, daffodil, crocus, and lily bulbs I continue to plant (usually too late) each fall. In their fleshy little selves lies an incipient beauty I can rely on to thrill me in the spring, even before I can get into the garden to do any of the revitalizing work that renews my spirit. Their perky, saucy, fresh faces sing me their chorus of joy and promise. I need that. It is indeed a miracle, and I know that God is in the garden.

Miracle-Gro and the Milky Way
Reconciling Science and Religion

when god decided to invent
everything he took one
breath bigger than a circustent
and everything began

when man determined to destroy
himself he picked the was
of shall and finding only why
smashed it into because

> E. E. Cummings, "when god
> decided to invent"

I am not an organic gardener. I feed the plants, trees, and shrubs in my garden with commercial chemical food supplements that sell under names such as Peters and Miracle-Gro, which are mixtures of varying percentages of nitrogen, phosphorus, and potash. Used correctly, they work;

the plants respond well to the chemical food poured on the soil around them.

Organic gardeners sneer at folks like me. They believe in getting food to their plants with natural materials such as kitchen scraps and animal manures added to their compost piles. Chicken manure is rich in nitrogen; well-rotted cow manure is high in phosphorus and potash. I admire the knowledge and commitment to purity of these people. Unquestionably, their approach to gardening is better for the overall environment than is mine. If I had the patience or the motivation to devote myself to learning what I would need to know, I think I might garden organically. But I don't, and if truth be told, I feel a little guilty about it. A little, but not enough to convince me to relinquish my reliance on the use of chemical supplements. Because I have great respect for organic gardening, though, I try to strike a compromise. I like to release into the garden natural predators such as ladybugs and praying mantises. They eat aphids and a host of other pests. Bats, encouraged to take up residence in a bat house or two placed strategically in various corners of the garden, are also a fine natural control for unwanted creepy crawlies.

Even the most passionate organic gardener must admit that science has done a lot to help gardeners, not only with the development of chemical plant foods but also with the creation of chemicals that can control all manner of pests — flying, creeping, crawling, burrowing. In a very real sense, gardening has itself become a science, and growers, especially professional growers, depend on scientific research. Growers now know exactly how long it takes for the seeds of various plants to germinate, and this knowledge enables them to time precisely plant development in their greenhouses. It is not magic that produces the abundance of seedling flats that tempt us each spring in nurseries. Plant biologists have revolutionized the nursery business, even as genetic engineering has revolutionized the growing of crops.

Science's stamp on our lives is ubiquitous and inescapable. It is hardly an exaggeration to suggest that science imprints every facet of our lives. The effect of science on what we grow and eat is just the tip of that iceberg. Whether and how we reproduce, how long we live or are kept alive, the quality of our lives, our mental and emotional health, our safety as individuals in a community, the way we are entertained, the ethical dilemmas that plague us — all are shaped by what science has created for us. Isn't it strange, then, that we seem willing, even eager, to embrace the changes that science offers us in every facet of our lives except one — religion? In this one area, millions of us seem so adamantly to refuse what various scientific disciplines tell us about how we got here, and how earlier civilizations, now long extinct, influenced written material we now hold sacred, that we are ready to go to social war with one another to defend what we want to believe, regardless of what science or the facts may reveal. A classic case in point is the continuing social war between evolutionists, who accept the biologists' and physicists' explanations of how the universe and its life have evolved since the big bang, and the creationists, who believe that the world came into being pretty much as described in the Book of Genesis.

EVOLUTION: THE DEAD DEBATE LIVES

One would have thought that debate would have been resolved long ago in the aftermath of the famous Scopes "monkey trial" of 1925, when Clarence Darrow and William

Jennings Bryan went head-to-head over the right of a public school teacher to teach the theory of evolution. Not so. Almost annually, somewhere in this country, someone or some group conducts a poll to ascertain what Americans believe about evolution, and not surprisingly, the results are usually quite similar.

In 1993, a Gallup poll revealed that almost half of all Americans believed that God created humans within the past ten thousand years. On January 19, 1997, the ever popular though hardly scientific *Parade* magazine reported that "75 percent of Americans cannot pass a basic National Science Foundation science quiz that asks questions like whether . . . humans and dinosaurs lived at the same time." Perhaps this lacuna in basic science knowledge is what leads to the desire to cling simultaneously to the two conflicting views of how the world came into being.

Seven years after the 1993 poll, the *New York Times* reported that a poll of fifteen hundred Americans conducted in March 2000 revealed that while 83 percent of those surveyed generally supported the teaching of evolution in public schools, 79 percent thought that creationism, presented as a belief rather than a scientific theory, should also be a part of the curriculum. David Haig, an evolutionary biologist at Harvard University, thought it "logically inconsistent both to believe in the theory of evolution, that humans did descend from animals, and to believe the opposite, that they were created in their present form." The March 2000 poll further indicated that about 30 percent of Americans believed that creationism should be taught as a scientific theory, either with or without evolution in the curriculum. Only 20 percent of those polled believed that evolution should be taught in science classes without any mention of creationism. The poll showed that young Americans ages eighteen to twenty-four and Americans with relatively high education levels were more likely to support teaching evolution and less likely to favor teaching creationism.

The astonishing fact is that today there are still states in the Union where only the theory of creationism is taught in the public schools. In Alabama, biology textbooks must carry a warning that reads in part, "No one was present when life first appeared on earth. Therefore, any statement about life's origins should be considered as theory, not fact." The specious logic of such a statement should be obvious to all. By such reasoning, one should also argue that because no one was atop Mount Sinai with Moses when he supposedly received the Ten Commandments from God, what is on those tablets should be seen as invalid. That being the case, why try to follow them as though they were a set of divine demands?

In 1996, the school superintendent of a conservative county in western Kentucky ordered that two pages explaining the big bang theory of cosmic origins in grade school textbooks be glued together. In August 1999, the Kansas state school board voted six to four to make the teaching of evolution optional rather than required. The board also deleted from its standards a description of the big bang theory. Steve Abrams, a member of the Kansas board who voted to make these changes, said that there were legitimate scientific doubts about whether the universe was more than several thousand years old. Steven Weinberg, a Nobel Prize–winning physicist, in his *Dreams of a Final Theory*, disagrees: "In conventional cosmological theories we can use the observed expansion rate of the universe to infer that the universe is about seven to twelve billion years old." So did the late Lewis Thomas, former president of the Memorial Sloan-Kettering Cancer Center in New York City and one of the nation's most distinguished medical scientists. "The planet formed as a solid oblate sphere and swung into its orbit roughly 4.7 billion years ago. Less than a billion years later, the first life appeared," Thomas wrote, in *The Fragile Species*. There simply is no doubt among scientists who know this field that the earth is more, much more than a few thousand years old. It is of more than passing interest that on March 11, 2000, the *New York Times* reported the discovery in Patagonia of the largest meat-eating dinosaur that ever walked the earth. According to Philip J. Currie, one of the two scientists who made the discovery, the species lived about 100 million years ago.

So here we are, three generations after the historic debate of the Scopes trial, and there are still places in this country where the teaching of evolution in our public schools is, if not banned outright, so degraded as to be ridiculed by those who continue to prefer, indeed insist on, teaching the young that the world as we know it actually came into being in the manner described in Genesis. That description is considered "factually correct" because it appears in the Bible, whereas evolution is considered only a theory because it lacks a "sacred base." This is the kind of euphemistic language that those who oppose the teaching of evolution love to use. But isn't the earth itself a "sacred base," vested with the glory and beauty of orderliness and law? Why, when it comes to religious belief, do we assume that only some written text contains truth, but not the physical world, which we can observe, explore, and test and where every season reveals its overwhelming truth: law and order, predictable, dependable, repeatable?

Can we be sure that the earth is really billions of years old and not just five thousand or ten thousand years old, as the creationists would have us believe? How do we know that life evolved from lower forms to higher forms over millions or billions of years, especially when we have no written record of the earth's antiquity? Dinosaur bones subjected to carbon 14 tests may not be sufficiently persuasive for those who feel their faith threatened by the thought of a world evolved rather than created by God in six days. Why does evolution so severely threaten that group of religionists we commonly call fundamentalists? Do they fear that their reasons for believing in the existence of God may be shattered by recognizing and accepting evolution as a correct description of how we got to where we are now? Perhaps, but I think that there is another, even more compelling reason for their rejection of evolution. From their perspective, it runs counter to biblical text, and since they are committed to the doctrine of biblical infallibility — a doctrine that teaches that every word in the Bible and the New Testament is God's unalterable, truly revealed word — to acknowledge the truth of evolution would be to deny the validity of the Bible.

ROCKS TELL THE STORY

One day soon after a visit to the American Museum of Natural History in New York City, where we had spent many hours looking at skeletons of all kinds and extinct animals that my grandchildren know the names of and I don't, one of them asked me this question: "Grandpa, how do we know, I mean really know, that the earth is old and how old the earth is?" We were out in the garden at the time, and I was digging a bed for some 'Bonica' rosebushes I wanted to put in beside a stone wall I had made. The digging was tough going. The glacier that millions of years ago swept over what is now known as New England left the area a rocky terrain. In fact, the spot where I was putting in this bed, two feet deep and twelve feet long, turned out to be God's own rock storage bin. It felt as though I was digging out a thousand pounds of rocks, and I cursed every one that my shovel hit.

"Rocks, Alex, rocks. That's how we know."

"Grandpa, quit digging. They're getting to you."

"No, no, they're not. Wait a minute." I ducked into the house and in a minute returned with a rock I had kept on my desk since the time I had served as a guest lecturer on the staff of a church camp in New Mexico. The site of the camp was renowned as a paleontological treasure trove, with one of the largest collections of fossilized rocks and petrified dinosaur skeletons in the nation, and visitors were allowed to wander through certain areas and even take home fragments. One afternoon, I found a rock with the perfect imprint of the skeleton of a small lizardlike creature, preserved in what is now stone but was at one time probably part of either a riverbed or a riverbank. We have all seen such fossilized rocks — in fact, slabs of this kind of fossilized stone are used as countertops or around bathroom sinks in many homes. So while it was hardly rare, this particular little rock had personal meaning for me because I had found it, and it also served as a reminder of the fact of evolutionary life.

"Here's your proof, young man. This small creature, forever entombed in this rock as a fossil, preceded the age of reptiles by maybe a million years. One layer of life development builds on the one previous, and we have physical evidence of all the various ages and stages of the development of life on earth. You saw some of it in the museum the other day. Spend more time there, learn what it has to show and teach, and you will understand not only the details of evolution but its meaning."

Brains evolved, as did bodies, and now the human brain has become our most important organ. We humans are the latest and most highly developed life form up to this moment on the evolutionary scale. We are the only life form fully aware of what transpires beyond our own immediate surroundings and capable of using that knowledge for purposes other than just our own survival. Through medicine and science, we can control the processes of evolution. We can adapt the environment to ourselves and our needs. Only humans have developed a conscience — that is, the ability to distinguish and choose between what we think is morally right and what is morally wrong. Moreover, only human beings can create great art, beautiful music, and eloquent poetry. Science and all the other disciplines of our intellect keep the refining process in flux.

LESSONS OF COSMOLOGY

If earth studies such as geology, paleontology, and archaeology show how life on earth evolved slowly from simple forms to more complex ones, a relatively new science, cosmology, confirms what the earth has revealed: this is a very old universe, and it is expanding. Despite some randomness, sometimes called chaos (a troubling and somewhat deceptive term), the laws governing the universe are very orderly and quite dependable. Each planet and star operates on a strict timetable. Astronomers can predict where any of them will be at any given moment. The fact of this precision is what allows us to predict tides and plan sea journeys with great accuracy, place people on the moon, land a spacecraft on Mars, and put space stations and satellites into orbit. Fresh water at sea level and motionless always freezes at 32 degrees Fahrenheit and boils at 212 degrees Fahrenheit. No exceptions. The science of chemistry is possible only because chemists can depend on chemical elements to behave the same way in every experiment.

Evidence of order in the universe is compelling, and that order is amazingly fine-tuned. In his book *Just Six Numbers: The Deep Forces That Shape the Universe*, Martin Rees, an English cosmologist, tells us:

> We cannot understand our origins without the cosmic context. The very hugeness of our universe, which seems at first to signify how unimportant we are in the cosmic scheme, is actually entailed by our existence! The expanse of space is not an extravagant superfluity; it is a consequence of the prolonged chain of events, extending back before our solar system formed, that preceded our arrival on the scene. . . . Supernovae have created the mix of atoms of which the earth is made. They are the building blocks for the intricate chemistry of life.

We are literally made of star stuff.

What is cosmology anyway? I wish I had a neat, simple definition, but I don't. Put all too simply, cosmology is the study of the origins of the universe, using the scientific disciplines of higher mathematics, nuclear physics, and astronomy to figure out how the cosmos and the tiny, finite speck called earth got here and survive. Cosmology also looks forward to speculate on the end of our universe, which is just one universe among millions. It is a relatively new science, little more than seventy years old, but in that short time, it has grown enormously in knowledge, owing in part to the development of highly specialized equipment such as the Hubble telescope and in even larger part to the increasingly sophisticated skills of scientists in all disciplines.

I first encountered cosmology during the summer of 1958, when by sheer chance I read a slim volume titled *Of Stars and Men* by the distinguished scientist Harlow Shapley, then a lecturer on cosmography at Harvard University. This work shattered my smug theology about humans being at the center of the universe and the ultimate goal of all creation, as well as my belief that evolution had some divine purpose. Yet somehow Shapley seemed to deepen my faith, giving it a totally different focus. I have never forgotten one of his most challenging rhetorical questions:

> If you were given the four basic entities and full power, opportunity, and desire, could you construct a universe like this one out of space, time, matter and energy? Or would you require a fifth entity — another basic property or action? . . . Is it a master entity, perhaps more basic . . . something quite unlike the four named above? Is it indispensable? Something that would make click a universe of stars, organisms, and natural laws that might otherwise be clickless?

Thus began a personal fascination with cosmology that has never waned. Over the forty or so years since I first opened *Of Stars and Men*, I have tried to immerse myself in cosmology, to learn and understand as much as I could about it. Yet the field has become so complex, so vast, so technical, so intense that I sometimes find myself drowning in it — feeling overwhelmed by a technocracy that my training has ill equipped me to understand.

Quantum mechanics and the Heisenberg uncertainty principle, both unknown prior to the end of the 1920s, lie at the heart of modern cosmological theory. These theories enable physicists to talk about a self-creating universe — a cosmos that erupts into existence spontaneously, much as a subnuclear particle sometimes pops out of nowhere in certain high-energy processes. Today most scientists agree that this is an accurate description of how our world was formed — out of the big bang. In 1951, Pope Pius XII, addressing the Pontifical Academy of Sciences in Rome on the implications of modern scientific cosmology, alluded to the big bang theory and the fact that "everything seems to indicate that the universe has in finite times a mighty beginning." Just what was this mighty beginning to which he alluded? Does Roman Catholicism accept the big bang as a way to describe how we got here?

THE BIG BANG

In his remarkable book *The First Three Minutes*, Steven Weinberg details this creative instant and what happened in the following moments:

> In the beginning there was an explosion . . . an explosion which occurred simultaneously everywhere. Practically instantaneously it filled all space, with every particle of matter rushing apart from every other particle. . . . At about one-hundredth of a second, the earliest time about which we can speak with any confidence, the temperature of the universe was about a hundred thousand million (10^{11}) degrees Centigrade. . . . None of the components of ordinary matter . . . could have held together. . . . The matter rushing apart in this explosion consisted of various types of the so-called elementary particles, which are the subject of modern high-energy

nuclear physics . . . electrons, positrons, neutrinos. . . .
These particles were continually being created out of
pure energy. . . . As the explosion continued the temperature dropped . . . until finally (at the end of the first
three minutes) it was cool enough for the protons and
neutrons to begin to form into complex nuclei. . . .

Eventually (after a few hundred thousand years of more cool-
ing) hydrogen and helium formed. A kind of primordial "soup"
developed.

Weinberg's description is confirmed by most other scientists, but Paul Davies adds to it the following important observation, in his *The Cosmic Blueprint*: "Cosmologists believe that
the Big Bang represents not just the appearance of matter and
energy in a pre-existing void, but the creation of space and
time too. The universe was not created *in* space and time;
space and time are *part of* the created universe." What an amazing concept! What Davies and others suggest is that the universe created itself. Is that possible?

The idea that something must have started it all off is
deeply ingrained in the minds of most of us and indeed is a
part of the world's culture. That "something" is usually understood as a creator, God. But was some sort of supernatural act
really necessary to have gotten our universe up and running?
It is in response to this age-old query that one finds the classic
disagreement between theologians and scientists. Religionists
have always needed to defend their traditional commitment
to a creator. Scientists see no such need. Religionists have
always been able to resort to the imagery, easy for everyone to
understand, of a great God who made the universe from nothing. (We set aside the difficulty of understanding how something can be made from nothing.) Scientists have had no such

easy imagery on which to rely. They have had the herculean task of trying to communicate complex and sophisticated physical and mathematical laws in order to persuade humanity that there is another, more accurate way of describing how it all began and developed.

The critical importance of the second law of thermodynamics in the process is a case in point. This law forbids heat to flow from cold bodies to hot ones, while allowing heat to flow from hot ones to cold ones. As the universe grows older, it grows colder. It is in a one-way, irreversible slide toward what scientists call a state of thermodynamic equilibrium, where eventually all matter will be in temperature balance. The fact that the universe is still seeking that universal temperature balance suggests that it cannot have endured eternally. It is this observation that has given rise to the big bang theory. After the initial massive explosion, the cosmos has continued to expand, with the galaxies rushing away from one another.

What caused the big bang in the first place? It was not the explosion of some concentrated lump of matter located at some particular place in a preexisting void. If only it were that easy. Compression is a more accurate response. Somewhere between ten billion and twenty billion years ago, the contents of the cosmos we see today were compressed into a minute volume of space. Einstein's theory of relativity teaches us that matter cannot be separated from time and space. As the compression intensified infinitely, the cosmos was squeezed into a single point, known to physicists as singularity. Time, space, and matter disappeared. And since laws of physics are formulated in terms of space and time, these laws, too, ceased to exist. If we ask where the big bang occurred, the answer is nowhere and everywhere. It did not occur at a point in space at all. Space came into existence with the big bang, as did time. What happened *before* the big bang? There was no *before*. Time began *with* the big bang. Strangely enough, this is exactly what Saint Augustine said in the fourth century when he reasoned that "the world and time had both one beginning. . . . The world was made, not in time, but simultaneously with time."

But did the big bang happen without a prior cause, and that cause without another prior cause, and so on until we get back to the traditional Prime Mover or Initial Cause? Quite possibly. Indeed, this probably was the case, at least according to the scientific thinking of quantum cosmologists — beginning with the German physicist Werner Heisenberg and extending through Max Planck, the originator of the quantum theory of physics, James Hartle, and Stephen Hawking. For such scientists, there is no origin of the universe. This does not mean, however, that the universe stretches back to infinity; existence without a beginning is as difficult to comprehend as creation out of nothing. Hawking, in *A Brief History of Time*, has put it this way: "So long as the universe had a beginning, we could suppose it had a creator. But if the universe is completely self-contained, having no boundary or edge, it would have neither beginning nor end: it would simply be. What place, then, for a creator?" It is here that quantum mechanics comes into play. At the heart of quantum physics lies the Heisenberg uncertainty principle, which states that all measurable quantities are subject to unpredictable fluctuations in their values. Thus the actual outcome of a particular quantum process is unknown and even, in principle, unknowable. The link between cause and effect is thus weakened.

What does all this imply? That the existence of the universe can be explained scientifically without the need for

God? Should we see the universe as a closed system, containing the reason for its existence entirely within itself? Given the laws of physics as we now know them, the universe can indeed take care of itself, including its own creation.

RELIGION IN A NEW ROLE

The implications of all this are profound — and, for some, profoundly troubling. It is time now for one and all to recognize that when it comes to describing how we, our world, our universe, our cosmos, got here, scientists do a better factual job than religionists, who have little if anything to say that adds to either the facts of creation or the factually based theories of it. Their wonderful stories are just that — wonderful and stories. At one time, people believed that those stories really did describe the way things happened. Now, under the impact of scientific discovery, religion has been forced to retreat from its exalted position as explainer of how the world originated. The process of describing just how it really happened began with Copernicus, Galileo, and Newton, but until now the forces of organized religion had either the power to repress or the authoritative position to ignore what science was telling the world. The pioneering work of astronomers such as Fred Hoyle and Edwin Hubble; physicists such as Stephen Hawking, John Wheeler, and Werner Heisenberg; and many others make that impossible now. They have reduced the mystery of the heavens by showing us that we are but one galaxy amid hundreds.

Evolutionary biologists show us how living things can evolve through natural selection. The retreat of religion from the ground now occupied by science is nearly complete;

religion ignores the discoveries of contemporary science at its own peril. If religion wants to continue to be a serious player in the shaping of human intellect, it will have to find ways to incorporate into its worldview what there is to be learned from the world of investigative science. Otherwise, it will run the risk of being little more than comfort food for the uncritical rank and file, dismissed as irrelevant by the knowledgeable. Those who think, teach, and speak in God's name need to find new ground to justify their existence and their right to humanity's equal time and attention. Some are struggling to do just that. A friend with whom I once had this discussion said to me, "I am willing to grant scientists all their theories. Although it would be nice to believe that there is some kind of divine plan in creation, my own theology does not depend on that. What remains unexplained is our constant striving for creativity, beauty, human love. These surely are beyond the realm of scientific explanation, and scientists have no greater claim to expertise in these areas than my tailor, butcher, baker, or candlestick maker." Philosophers, poets, writers, and artists can rightfully claim equal expertise in explaining the desires of the human heart. The artist, especially in his or her struggle to express the abstract and to understand and evoke emotion, gives reality and meaning to the existence of what we call the spirit. Composers such as Mozart and Beethoven add more than mere color to our cosmos; they deepen its meaning.

Scientists also understand this quest for meaning. With great caution, yet without derision, they approach the question of order in the universe and its meaning. Thus Paul Davies wrote in *The Cosmic Blueprint:*

> That the universe has organized its own self-awareness is for me powerful evidence that there is something going on behind it all. The impression of design is overwhelm-

ing. Science may explain all the processes whereby the universe evolves its own destiny, but that still leaves room for there to be meaning behind existence.

And Harold Fritzsch says, in *The Creation of Matter*:

> What about the existence of God in our world of science? Is there room for God in a world that seemingly can dispense with His intervention in the processes of the universe? . . . Are religion and science an irreconcilable contradiction? I do not believe that such a contradiction exists nor ever existed. This intuitive sense for the unity of the universe in my opinion warrants the designation *religiosity*.

Science is not necessarily religion's enemy, except insofar as religion — fearful of the weakness of its own argument for God from a classic, unreasoned basis and therefore more assertive, more defensive than necessary — makes science an enemy by denying, ignoring, or degrading its findings.

MYTHS AND TRUTHS

What, then, shall we do with the mythic tales in the Bible, especially the creation story found in Genesis, chapters 1 and 2? When one thinks about it, it is these chapters, more than any others, that have set the scientific viewpoint at odds with the religious one.

I have been teaching about how the Hebrew Bible came into being for more than forty years. I have taught this material at the college level, in adult education settings, and to children and teenagers. Regardless of the age group involved,

I always begin with the same sentence: "The Bible is the most dangerous book in the world." My point is that a simple reading of the first eleven chapters of Genesis can make an agnostic, if not an atheist, out of anyone who has ever taken an introductory course in biology, physics, astronomy, or, for that matter, the history of the Middle East. As you might expect, people are taken aback by this statement, especially coming from a rabbi — a teacher of and believer in Divinity. I have seen the bristles of hostility rise on the necks of hundreds: How could he say such a thing? What does he mean? Blasphemy.

I begin with such a threatening assertion precisely because anyone who has ever been exposed to ancient history, biblical criticism, archaeology, or any of the sciences knows that the first eleven chapters of Genesis are myths that may — and I believe do — reveal great moral and ethical truths, but not factual truths. There is a great difference between the two. "Two plus two equals four" is a fact that can be proved and replicated. So can the assertion that water is a combination of two parts hydrogen and one part oxygen. That the earth revolves around the sun and not vice versa is also a fact, one that religious authorities militantly opposed for fifteen hundred years before it was accepted. But the Garden of Eden story, the story of Noah building an ark to save animal and human lives, and the Tower of Babel story do not fall into the category of factual truths. They are myths, found initially in Sumerian, Assyrian, or Babylonian literature. These civilizations dominated the Middle East as much as two thousand years before the biblical period. The Akkadian tale of Gilgamesh closely parallels the biblical Flood tale, except that in the former, the efforts of Gilgamesh, the hero of the story, end in failure, whereas in the biblical tale, Noah and his family survive to continue the human line. We have thousands of fragments of those earlier myths. The clay tablets on which they were written have been dug up by archaeologists, and as a result, we now know the sources from which the biblical writers drew their material. We can also assume how and why they made changes in those earlier legends: to teach the moral truths they wanted their people to accept and believe in. They made a distinction between truth-fact and truth-meaning. We need to learn from them how to make that distinction.

There are actually two creation stories in the first two chapters of Genesis. They stand in sharp contrast to each other. In one, man and woman are made at the same time (Gen. 1:27–28); in the second, woman is fashioned from man's rib (Gen. 2:21–22). Why the two differing stories in the same sacred text? There is wide speculation. Clearly, the latter is drawn from an earlier Sumerian story that told of Nin-ti, meaning either "lady of the rib" or "lady of life," hence the name Eve for the biblical woman, a name that in Hebrew means "life." The biblical writers were not too deeply troubled by the inconsistency between these two versions. As already noted, they were pursuing moral meaning, not factual truth.

The critical text in the creation story is found in chapter 2, verse 7 of Genesis: "Then the Lord God formed man from the dust of the earth, He blew into his nostrils the breath of life, and man became a living soul." No other living creature is described as having been ensouled in this or any other way. They just live. Humankind, on the other hand, is enlivened by divine breath. That makes human beings unique, special, sacred. The implications are enormous. People are to be regarded and treated differently from other living creatures. If a murderer should take the life of another human being illegally or immorally, he or she would pay a penalty that would not be paid for any other kind of life taking. The biblical writer wished to convey a profound truth: human beings are possessed of God's spirit and must, therefore, be treated with the utmost respect and care. This is the message of the first two chapters of Genesis. Not bad. And as I read of our increasing insensitivity toward one another, I am convinced that it needs constant and forceful reiteration. Religion has its task cut out for it.

RELIGION AND SCIENCE

Some people are upset with science not because they believe that it is factually wrong (it isn't), but because they believe that it has robbed the universe of all mystery and purpose. By mystery, they must mean mystique, the intriguing quality of the unknown. Of mystery, the as yet unsolved or unexplained in the universe, there is still plenty — plenty of the unknown, of the as-yet-to-be-discovered in cosmic and worldly life. Has science robbed the cosmos of purpose? That question is far more difficult to answer. Does our universe contain or reflect some cosmic or divine purpose? The categories of rational human thought cannot definitively answer that question, but the physicist Freeman Dyson, quoted in Davies's *The Mind of God*, once said, "I do not feel like an alien in this universe." Purpose enough? For some.

Unfortunately, the need to defend the biblical myths as factually correct, lest one's faith be shown to be somehow lacking, has needlessly pitted science and religion against each other. We start defending or attacking the literal texts rather than asking what spiritual idea the writer wanted us to glean from the story. Charles Darwin's *Origin of Species* threatened a religious community that up to that point in history had had only its own faith to shape it. The tools of biblical criticism, archaeology, and modern-day cosmology were not yet available to biblical scholars, theologians, and religious historians. Now they are, and because they are, science and religion no longer need to repudiate each other to justify themselves. Instead, they can complement each other. The science of the cosmos can indeed strengthen, if not confirm, the faith of the believer. For such a person, the heavens do show the glory of God. Cosmology need not destroy that belief. There is a remarkable parallelism between what goes on in a primal wetland and what takes place in the starry universe. As we see the one mirrored in the other and consider the orderliness of both, the leap of faith becomes smaller.

I am impressed by the humility of many astronomers, cosmologists, and scientists who study the vastness of our cosmos and its interaction with earth. They reflect an awe that borders on the spiritual. As you read their words, you discover that in many instances, science strengthens our all-too-human will to believe. Paul Davies concluded his book *The Mind of God* this way:

> I cannot believe that our existence in this universe is a mere quirk of fate, an accident of history, an incidental blip in the great cosmic drama. Our involvement is too intimate. The physical species *Homo* may count for nothing, but the existence of mind in some organism on some planet in the universe is surely a fact of fundamental significance. Through conscious beings the universe has generated self-awareness. This can be no trivial detail, no minor byproduct of mindless, purposeless forces. We are truly meant to be here.

Many a warm summer night, I venture out to the garden and, seated in one of my comfortable Adirondack chairs, lean back and watch the night sky in its dazzling performance. The vastness and complexity of the Milky Way astonish and overwhelm me. That astronomers, cosmographers, and some physicists know each and every star and planet in that huge heavenly highway leaves me breathless. That what I can see is only one galaxy in a cosmos whose galaxies number ten to the twentieth power humbles me absolutely. One does not need a telescope and a degree in astronomy to stand in awe before the orderliness evident in our natural world and in the starry heavens that envelop it.

I also find that order in my garden. There, too, law and order are evident. In both spaces, celestial and terrestrial, science has added immeasurably to our knowledge, our understanding, and our enjoyment. For both spaces, science has given us the tools to increase our productivity. It has allowed us to penetrate space, even as it has enabled us to create finer varieties of lilies, chrysanthemums, and corn. Could we continue without this wonderful tool called science? Of course we could. We could also survive without cars, computers, or spacecraft. Could we continue without the help modern science brings to our knowledge of the past? Yes, we could. Is it in our interest, or in the interest of generations unborn, to live wearing such blinders? I think not. Here is another place where I and the fundamentalists part company. And now you know why I feel only a *little* guilty when I use Miracle-Gro in my garden.

A Life Lesson from the Peonies

Patience is power, with time and patience
the mulberry leaf becomes silk.

Chinese proverb

T here are two kinds of peonies — deciduous and tree.
While their flowers may appear to be similar, their
natures and growing patterns are very different. Tree peonies
grow on a hard stem, like a small tree trunk. Also like a tree,
they lose their leaves in the fall, but the stem remains and next
year's buds grow on it. In time, this annual process results in a
bush that can become quite large. A mature tree peony can
grow four to five feet tall.

A deciduous peony, on the other hand, grows from a root
or tuber, dies back to the ground at the end of each growing
season, and seems to disappear. But miraculously, it reappears

each year in the spring. If healthy, and under normal growing conditions, the tuber will multiply and put out increasingly more and larger shoots. That is what accounts for a deciduous peony's growth. It is this variety of peony with which most people are familiar, while the tree peony — considerably larger, far more delicate, and with much more beautiful flowers — remains a mystery to the majority of Westerners. Asians know tree peonies quite well, and in fact, their growth is almost revered in Eastern cultures.

Deciduous peonies bloom in my garden around the end of May, and I can never get enough of them. There is nothing quite so appealing, quite so satisfying as a bowl of freshly cut peonies in the house. They fill the room with their perfume. The French Impressionist Pierre Auguste Renoir seemed to have been captivated by them, for he brilliantly, uniquely captured their soft pastel colors — pink, white, even bicolor — in his paintings, especially in his portraits of young girls and women. Little wonder that novice and expert alike are drawn to planting peonies in their gardens. A bed of peonies in full bloom in some sunny garden spot can satisfy all the senses.

I well remember my earliest ventures into peony cultivation. Like most beginners, I started with the deciduous variety. I had not even heard of tree peonies at the time; the planting and care of those beauties would come much later. Because it is much cheaper to order peony tubers from catalogs than it is to buy containerized plants from the nursery, I scoured the catalogs for those I thought most beautiful. The varieties are truly dazzling.

The roots arrived in early fall, in perfect condition. I hurried them into their prepared bed, carefully following the instructions (actually more like dire warnings): eyes, the whitish buds of the root, to be planted no more than an inch and a half to an inch and three-quarters — certainly no more than two inches — below the surface. If they were planted any deeper, I was warned, the plants might never bloom. Peonies, it seems, are fussy critters. I added a handful or two of bonemeal to the planting hole, covered the roots with topsoil, marked each plant, and, with a feeling of accomplishment and satisfaction, sat back. Soon — that is, the next spring, so I thought — my garden bed would mirror the beguiling catalog display, and my senses would be gratifyingly overwhelmed. Little did I know.

That first summer, the roots I had planted the previous fall produced healthy-looking plants, a lot of leaves, and absolutely no flowers, not even buds. Being herbaceous, they died back that fall and disappeared into the ground. I assumed that they were dead and gone. But early the next spring, while poking around the garden bed, I noticed some little red stalk tips beginning to shoot through the soil where I remembered I had planted the peonies. By late April, they had developed into good-size stalks, and by May large leaves graced the stems. No buds, though, and no blooms. Where had I gone wrong? What had I done or not done? More than a bit disappointed, I went on to other things, writing off peony cultivation as a bad experiment.

The third spring, I again noticed those by now familiar red spikes poking through the ground, only now they seemed to be growing with fierce abandon. At each planting place, massive clumps of red nodes appeared in a cluster. By late April, vigorous plants bushed out, and on each stalk hordes of ants climbed over gum-ball-size flower buds, which by May burst into a display that left me breathless. My peony bed bloomed beyond my wildest imagination and has continued to do so annually ever since. The house and that bed now belong to someone else, but I showed the new owner the location of the peony bed. Whenever I see her (our paths do cross from time to time), she raves about the peonies and seems to enjoy them as much as we did.

My tree peonies have gone through the same slow cycle of growth. Some have been in place and blooming for more than fifteen years. They are now quite large, some with branches so burdened with blooms in the spring that they need shoring up from below. The blossoms on some of them measure eight to ten inches across. One, named 'Souvenir Maxim Cornu', I call my bashful bloomer. It produces huge, golden yellow blossoms with burnt umber centers that hang down under the leaves and have to be lifted to be seen. It is well worth the effort. What splendor!

THE LESSON OF PATIENCE

I have learned something from peony culture that all gardeners come to know: patience. You must be patient if you want to enjoy the enormous beauty peonies offer. In time, they will pour out their hearts for you, but it does take time. There is a little phrase gardeners delight in using: sleep, creep, and leap. The first year you put a perennial plant in the ground, it creeps along, growing slowly. The second year, it does a little better, but still not enough to satisfy. The third year, it positively leaps out at you with its furious growth and bloom.

I think about that phrase in connection with today's culture, which hardly lends itself to the patience required for peony growing. We are an impatient society. We want it all, and we want it *now*. Instant gratification is the curse of the contemporary world.

Strange as it may seem, I am particularly reminded of this when I walk into a hospital room filled with flowers or potted plants sent by family and friends. These plants have been raised in professional greenhouses, their blooms forced. They are weak and tender plants that ordinarily do not survive for long. Easter is a season especially notorious for this problem. As if by magic, azaleas, huge pots of Martha Washington geraniums, and, of course, calla lilies suddenly appear in nurseries and on the streets in front of florist shops. What nicer way to celebrate the twin spring holidays of Easter and Passover than by giving plants, the gift of spring. But if truth be told, these plants are fated to wilt, having also been forced for the season in professional greenhouses. If gathered up right after their moment in the holiday sun and treated tenderly, however, they can be a gardener's treasure trove.

I have developed a sneaky habit. On visiting the hospital rooms of my congregants, I often notice the condition of the potted plants given to them. If they (the plants, not the patients) seem to be spent and on the slippery slope to plant heaven, I become brazen: "Since that azalea is dying anyway, mind if I take it and put it in my garden? If it makes it, it will remind me of your recovery." The request usually works like a charm, and I have picked up a lot of tired plants that way. I leave the hospital room feeling better for the visit. Gardening aside, that is what a visit to the sick usually does for the visitor. In Judaism, such a visit is considered a good deed, a mitzvah.

As a result of my hospital visits, the small greenhouse I had on my terrace began to bulge with expiring azaleas. Water, warmth, a good trimming, and a heavy dose of Miracid kept them on botanical life support until I could get them out to the country and into the warming spring soil. Half would make it through the summer. Come fall, I would cover those that did survive with a thick blanket of leaves and a passing prayer of hope. Then wait! Spring arrived and finally the ground thawed. I would dash out to my "waiting room." Voilà! Ever so lightly, I would scratch the bark of the surviving plants with my thumbnail to see if there was any green underneath. If so, I would replace their leaf blanket. Wait. Patience. It was not yet time. It was still too cool.

My success rate was not high, but more than a few made it, and now each year they remind me of Harry or Rose or Henry, from whom years earlier I had filched the plant. Good to report that for the most part, Harry, Rose, and Henry are also fully recovered and doing well. Again, the garden has taught me a lesson. Matters cannot be forced. Things — be they nature, relationships, or ideas — need time to mature. There is a rhythm to matters that must be perceived, appreciated, and cultivated. Hamlet was correct when he observed, "There's a divinity that shapes our ends." We need to find that rhythm. Doing so takes time and patience.

We probably cannot teach this to the young. Their hormones and their age work against their learning such lessons. But adults should not be children in their approach to life, to relationships, to faith, to God. I am amazed at how we ignore the obvious lesson of the need for patience in our everyday lives. We seem to be possessed by the need to have the newest now. It is not only our acquisitive habits that reflect this tendency. We eat this way, too. Fast-food outlets of every variety spoil our roadways and byways. We eat on the fly, or we take out and take it home. Some purveyors of what we have learned to call junk food deliberately fill their offerings with the kinds of fats and spices they know will appeal to those who for one reason or another want and seem to need the instant gratification that food brings. There have been reams of studies on what eating like this does to our health — none of it good.

WE WANT RELIGION,
AND WE WANT IT RIGHT NOW

We seem to be carrying our need for instant gratification into our faith systems as well. The growing popularity of Pentecostal and Evangelical worship styles may be a reflection of this need: "Get saved *now!*" "Find God *now!*" Religious institutions seem to be promising instant salvation, spontaneous redemption, and the emotionally releasing style of worship that so often accompanies these promises furthers the desire for instant satisfaction that will brighten all too often otherwise dreary lives.

Evangelical and Pentecostal churches are the fastest-growing religious institutions in America. While most mainline Protestant denominations are struggling to survive, the Southern Baptist Convention, Assembly of God, Churches of God, Pentecostal and Holiness groups, Evangelicals, Mormons (Church of Jesus Christ of Latter-day Saints), and Jehovah's Witnesses are overflowing with vitality and expanding memberships.

Why the new popularity? Why the explosive growth? Surely, it is not because of their liberal social philosophies or rational intellectual theologies. Pentecostals don't have a creed or even a single denomination. Rather than being written down in a single volume, their theology is diffused among their songs, prayers, sermons, and testimonies, which challenge the secular worldview. They are not particularly tolerant of other church groups, nor do they think much in ecumenical terms. In fact, they often refuse to recognize the validity of other faiths' teachings. They try to impose uniformity of belief and practice on members by censorship, even in some cases heresy trials. The Southern Baptist Convention once tried to withdraw from its own publishing house a biblical commentary that it deemed too liberal. The Lutheran Church–Missouri Synod raised more than a few eyebrows some years back when its president undertook a personal investigation of one of its seminaries to find and expel faculty members whose teachings were not compatible with those of the church. How can such groups experience the popularity they now seem to enjoy?

The response to this question begins, I believe, in understanding that first and foremost, people are "meaning seekers." They want their lives to have meaning, and when they do not, despair and a sense of futility take over, often with disastrous consequences. People instinctively seek lifestyles and institutions that express the opposite of these negative feelings. Evangelical faith allows its adherents to find meaning in their suffering by focusing on and committing themselves to their God, who is portrayed as one prepared to bear their burdens. Moreover, these groups provide enormous socialization opportunities, through which both pain and joy are shared. A successful religious organization is one in which there is a stream of shared experience among a continuing community of adherents who also share the same beliefs. A successful religion is one that explains life effectively for its members. In an age of alienation, with people living anonymously in compacted areas of high population density, a place where anonymity and loneliness can be overcome under the mantle of a commonly shared experience is bound to hold a strong attraction.

When a handful of wholly committed people give themselves fully to a faith or cause, they can be virtually irresistible, for a number of reasons: (1) They are willing to put more time and effort into their cause than most people. (2) They have an assurance, a conviction of rightness, of being on the side of God, that the less faithful cannot match. (3) They are linked together in a band of mutually supportive, like-minded, equally devoted fellow believers, who reinforce one another in times of weakness, pain, persecution, or doubt. (4) They are willing to subordinate their personal desires and ambitions to the shared goals of the group. Evangelical and Pentecostal churches satisfy all of these conditions.

In his book *Fire from Heaven,* the well-known Harvard Divinity School professor and writer Harvey Cox suggests that in failing to supply people with solutions to overwhelming social problems and in failing to supply society with a sense of lasting meaning, secular culture — and, I would add, mainstream religious groups — paradoxically triggered a religious renaissance. Cox sees Pentecostalism as the most dramatic expression of God's revenge against the "God is dead" theology. And in its almost primitive spirituality, he also sees a protest against an existing religious language that has lost its force. Cox believes that in the twentieth century, American Protestantism, as well as Judaism, became increasingly desacralized or rationalistic and concerned with social issues. Voting with their feet, many people left mainstream religion for the fervent spirituality still often cherished in more orthodox religions, as well as in Pentecostalism. As a result, we are seeing an enormous change in what people expect from religion, even as we are seeing the Protestant religion change. Americans question secular materialism (even though they enjoy its comforts, its goodies, its benefits) and religious dogma. They prefer the intuitive as a source of validity, even truth.

A similar revolution is visible in America's Jewish community, currently in the midst of an exciting and unexpected renaissance as a result of the same kind of impatience with any and all stagnant religious models. But — and this is the unforeseen part — American Jews are not impatient with the old if it is authentic and can be used to further their quest for what they view as spirituality. Jewish students at many of the country's most secular colleges and universities are less religiously rationalistic than their parents. More than ever before in American life, young Jews who are going to synagogues are going to ones where the worship style is best described as "swinging" — filled with rhythmic music, dancing, and hand clapping — and where the emphasis is on participatory group prayer, more often in Hebrew than in English. Even those who are not synagogue-oriented — and they make up the majority — are interested in exploring the mystical aspects of their religious traditions. Today they are far more serious about their heritage as Jews than they have ever been before, even though this may not express itself in weekly synagogue attendance. The young feel vulnerable and have a touching need for something on which to rely. They want to learn what their ancestors did, said, and believed and how they preserved their identity in the face of terrible, relentless persecution. Surprisingly, they are using study as a vehicle to explore these new directions. But, of course, study has always been a form of worship in Jewish life.

PATIENCE: A REQUIREMENT OF FAITH

Professor Burton Visotzky teaches in New York at the Jewish Theological Seminary, the training ground for Conservative Judaism's rabbis. He is also well known as a participant in the select group that a few years ago, with Bill Moyers as host, explored the Book of Genesis on a popular public television series. An astute interpreter of the new approach to the search for meaning and spirituality that is now so much a part of religious life in this country, Visotzky sees religion as "a constant struggle to learn. The study of Torah (a word used here to describe the totality of Judaism's written past) is the one commandment that has no parameters. We're obligated to do it all the time, as long as we live." In Winifred Gallagher's *Working on God*, Visotzky, referring to the practice of reading the entire first five books of the Hebrew Bible in the synagogue in regular weekly sections, observes:

> We read Torah each year. The words are the same but we've changed, so the text has whole new layers of meaning. The rabbis say, "Turn it and turn it, all things are in it." I used to think they meant that if one looked at the jewel of Torah from enough angles, one would finally understand it. Now, I think they meant that if you just keep turning and turning, the text will always serve you.

In the synagogue and in the classroom, worship and study are communal. At any given Sabbath worship service, the biblical portion of the week will be read and the rabbinic commentaries associated with it will be described and discussed by a qualified leader, usually the congregation's rabbi, as part of the liturgy. In many synagogues today, regardless of whether they are liberal or more traditional in style, a similar process is followed at a Torah study session held before the worship service. This communal approach to expounding and explaining the Torah makes it difficult to distinguish between study and prayer. In a classroom during the week, two students will together study various religious material, including Torah text and its commentaries, "cross-pollinating" each other with their interpretations and understanding of the material, much the way bees work in the garden. This centuries-old method of study, commonly used in the Jewish schools and communities of Europe in the days prior to World War II, is now being revived and successfully transposed into a contemporary setting here in America.

Studying with a partner has many virtues, not the least of them that it keeps both students intellectually honest. It is a wonderful way to learn, but it is a slow process. It takes time, as students argue back and forth, defending their positions vigorously and with constant reference to the particular text. Insights or truths gleaned from the Torah may suddenly emerge, but this is different from some instantaneous revelation. The former emerge as a result of a diligent process, patiently applied, slowly and painstakingly, the way one builds a garden slowly over the years. Whether done in this *chevruta** style or by regular classroom methods, study is fundamental and basic to Judaism. It is a never-ending process, and it takes time. It is the gardening pathway to faith. The rabbis tell us that an ignorant man cannot be a pious man.

Judaism does not place a great deal of reliance on the instantaneous conversion, the flash of revelation. It does not deny that such moments can and do occur, but it is not Judaism's usual way. A popular slogan inscribed over the arks in many of our synagogues is *Da lifney me atah omed* (Know before whom thou standest). The emphasis is on the word

---

*This word comes from the Hebrew word *chaver*, meaning "friend." As early as the first century, the rabbis admonished one and all to acquire a friend for the purpose of study.

know. It is not meant to suggest that we know God fearfully and humble ourselves in dread before the Divinity, so much as it is a reminder that knowledge is the critical way to understanding God. *Know* in this context means "search out" — search for God with all your skills — intellectual, emotional, experiential — so that you may understand the Eternal One as completely as possible. Knowing does not rule out the joyous. To the contrary: there is a vast structure within Judaism called Hasidism, which emphasizes the expression of Judaism through joy. It is very popular, and deservedly so. The psalmist admonishes us to "serve the Lord with gladness" (Ps. 100:2). The Hasidim have elevated that commandment to an exciting art form that has survived for two centuries and from which all of us can learn today.

Hasidism is not Pentecostalism. Neither is it Evangelical. It is within Judaism's mainstream, and what distinguishes it is its joyous fervor. Non-Hasidic forms of contemporary Judaism are striving now to incorporate more of the upbeat Hasidic style into their music and liturgical practices. Such efforts are commendable, and I believe they should be encouraged. For too long, Jews at worship, especially Reform Jews, looked not so much like God's chosen people, but more like God's frozen people. Congregational participation was reduced to a minimum. Congregants came to the synagogue to be sung to and preached at. Little wonder that attendance declined over the years. Mainstream Protestantism suffered much the same fate. Its style was formal, genteel, refined, and somewhat dull, but it has now adopted a more participatory pattern. Who knows, maybe the *chevruta* style of worship will catch on in Protestant churches as well. Imagine the congregation studying the weekly New Testament selection instead of just listening to it being read.

The Evangelical or Pentecostal style may work for some communities on an emotional level, but it may not be as effective for those used to a more cerebral approach. It's true that religion may be enjoyed and expressed through the highly emotive, but I do not think it can really grow that way. Faith must be shaped by more than emotional moments. Instantaneous salvation, faith in a flash, throwing oneself into God's hands and hoping for the best, is neither right nor wrong. It just strikes me as being insufficient as a building block for a mature religious life. A sustaining faith demands more and should get more and better from us. I see faith as a commitment to the sum total of beliefs, sentiments, and practices, individual and social, that has as its object a power we recognize as supreme, on which we depend for guidance and inspiration, and with which, through prayer and ethical conduct, we can enter into a relationship. Such a faith is arrived at only after much effort, struggle, thought, and behavior refined by social experience. It requires patience and experimentation. Faith is a process in becoming. Working to achieve it never ends.

Many times, at the end of a day in the garden, as I am putting away my tools and sweeping up the remnants of the mess I have left about, I look around and say to myself, "I will never finish it. I will never get it just right." And then I am reminded of what a wise teacher in our tradition left us: "It is not incumbent on you to finish the task, but neither are you free to desist from beginning it."

A garden is like that. It is never finished. Faith is like that. It is never complete. It is always a process, a growing, a discarding, an adding of the new.

One year, I spent nearly $50 for a very special peony root. I found myself muttering, "You must be crazy." I need not tell you that I planted that peony in a very special, very protected, well-marked place and gave it huge doses of tender loving care. True to form, it took three years to bloom properly. It was worth the wait. Its flowers are bloodred. Its unusual foliage is feathery. It blooms for about a week and then dies back, disappearing from the garden by the middle of June. Its appearance is brief but oh so beautiful. Each year I wait patiently for *Paeonia fenus folia* to make its appearance. Patience. Someone once said it is a virtue. Perhaps.

Patience has a long history in our tradition. Noah waited out the Flood. No easy task, given the crowded conditions of the ark and the nature of its passengers. The writer of the Song of Songs urged us to be patient for love: "Stir not up love until it pleases" (Song of Songs 2:7). The psalmist cautioned us to "wait patiently for the Lord" (Ps. 27:14). The prophet Habakkuk warned us to wait patiently for redemption: "Though it tarry, wait for it" (Hab. 2:3). The first-century rabbi Hillel in his wisdom cautioned, "An impatient man is not fit to be a teacher."

Surely, I can wait for a peony to mature and bless me with its fragrant blossoms. And just as surely, we can all learn to curb our acquisitive habits and our seemingly insatiable desire to have it all and to have it *right now.*

The Garden Bench

"Free at last! Free at last!
Thank God Almighty, we are free at last!"

*Negro spiritual, quoted by
Martin Luther King Jr.*

I f the cultivation of peonies helped me deepen my understanding of the value of patience, the garden bench my companion, Marcia, gave me for Father's Day taught me a different but equally important lesson. Like so much of what happens when you're gardening, the sudden presence of a new bench in my garden served as a catalyst for new thoughts and insights. And in a strange way, it led me to some wisdom from my own religious and cultural roots.

I have discovered that nowadays when I am "out there," as Marcia describes the garden, I find myself wanting to sit down for a minute or two. Since that is a relatively new fact of my life, a bench comfortably and strategically placed is a very pleasant convenience. After an hour or so of fighting the shovel, the pitchfork, and (in the instance I am about to describe) a couple of tons of newly delivered Pennsylvania quarry stone, these older bones, joints, and muscles cry out for a rest.

Some time ago, I came across an article on fitness in one of those magazines that find their way to folks like me — the over-sixty-five crowd. It prescribed exercise for the "modern mature" and gave a list of activities with the calorie-loss value neatly noted next to each workout. As expected, biking and jogging were at the top of the list. Gardening was somewhere down in the lower half, lost in the category labeled "mild forms of exercise." The estimated calorie loss from a couple of hours in the garden was negligible.

Mild form of exercise indeed. Because I am an inveterate "Letters to the Editor" writer (almost all of which never get published), my first inclination was to dash off a letter to that magazine, inviting whoever wrote the piece to my house any spring or fall to work with me for a day. The writer could follow me as I hauled a ton of topsoil from the delivery truck two hundred yards away to the new bed I was digging, or as I started to carve a new garden out of a former woods, first cutting down the trees, then digging the stumps, and finally rototilling the cleared and well-fertilized space. If, after any or all of that activity, said writer had any energy left, I might let him or her share the light duty — popping the plant material into the prepared beds. Mild form of exercise indeed.

The entrance to our house was originally achieved by walking up a slope — not too steep, not too long, but definitely a bit of a pitch. In wet weather or in snow, that little climb posed a bit of a problem, especially for very young children or for anyone carrying packages. I managed to eliminate that by setting in some broad steps, bordered by railroad ties and filled with gravel, to ease people into the house. But the area beside the steps remained an ugly slope that in spring and fall tended to become a mini-Niagara as the rainwater poured off the hill. "So build a retaining wall," one of my clever friends suggested one summer evening as we stood around, glasses in hand. Like seed in potting soil, the idea took root.

I am not good at landscape design. I have taken a couple of courses to improve my "conceptualization capacity," but I am still relatively unimaginative when it comes to envisioning an area properly landscaped. Thankfully, the Berkshires, where we live and garden, are blessed with many excellent landscape designers. Matt is one of the best; he can do amazing things with the placement of rocks and boulders, and I envy those skills. He had done the preliminary design around the house when it was first built, but it had been years since we had last seen or talked to him. So I called him, and the next day he came over with his marking wheel, clipboard, and design pencil.

"You need a two-tiered retaining wall," he said. "Make it out of Pennsylvania quarry stone. That will take the curse off the slope and give you two nice, level planting areas. You can fill the upper tier with a lovely specimen needle tree and the lower with some bulbs and perennials. It will add a good measure of interest to the entryway. Call the stone yard. They have the stone and will deliver. You need a couple of pallets. And make sure you dig a two-foot trench to hold the base stones. Tie the wall back into the slope. Don't forget to put a gravel fill down in the trenches before you drop in the big base stones. Here, I'll leave you a sketch." A cup of coffee and some welcome advice about how to treat other parts of the garden completed our conversation, and Matt was gone.

To this day, I do not know whether Matt expected me to call a stonemason to build that wall or thought I would take it on as a kind of do-it-yourself weekend project. Thirty years earlier, I had built a very small, amateurish retaining wall beside the garage entrance to my old house on Martha's Vineyard. That hardly qualified me for this project. The location of that old wall made it practically invisible. This one was to be at the entrance to the house, directly in the eyes of God and man.

"I'm going to build it myself," I announced to Marcia. I'll refrain from describing the look on her face as I said this. But what did *she* know? I might have asked as well, what did I know?

The huge flatbed delivery truck, with a forklift built on, backed up the drive at about 7:00 A.M. "Don't these guys ever sleep?" I said to myself. I watched as the driver/operator shoved the forks of the lift into the bottom of each of the pallets and swung them no more than three feet over the roof of my car, depositing them ever so gently on the side of the drive opposite the slope. At least a ton or two (or three or four) of good-size rocks — some weighing more than a hundred pounds, I was soon to discover — now blocked the top of the drive.

I cut away the wire mesh holding the rocks to the pallet and stared. Building a rock wall, I realized, requires more than a little imaging technique. One has to be able to see where a rock belongs. Unless one wants to lift any given stone more than once, it is best to envision the rock in place before moving it. Building a rock wall also requires plain old ordinary brute strength, especially when dropping the big base stones into their places in the trenches. I followed Matt's instructions to the letter. Believe me, that wall of mine is not about to move from frost or winter thaw.

By the end of the second morning, I could barely stand up as I got out of bed. By the end of the first week, I had dropped stones on most of my fingers. I could tell by their color that the nails on two of them would soon be a part of history. By the end of the second week, the wall was complete, and good soil from my compost pile was in place in the new two-tiered beds. In time, we picked out the right tree, a 'Morris Blue' pine, and because of its size had it planted. The bulbs and perennials were easy to set in.

What an enormous sense of accomplishment. All that work, but it was worth every ache, every soreness, every minute of the labor expended. Is it a great wall? I would not want a professional wall builder to critique it too severely. Does it work? Yes. Am I proud of it? You bet. Would I do it again? In a heartbeat. In fact, I am planning to build a small retaining wall around one of the ponds in the woodland garden I'm now designing. At least now I have learned some of the tricks. (Wear heavy gloves.)

Don't tell me that gardening is not labor-intensive. I have learned something important about work — and rest. As I think about it, what I learned the hard way, our ancestors knew centuries ago. Why don't we learn from them and practice what their legacy has given us?

THE DIGNITY OF LABOR

Unlike the cultures of ancient Greece or Rome, Judaism placed a very high premium on labor and the dignity of work. Strange, particularly when one finds the practice of slavery so deeply embedded in biblical life. The Hebrew Bible is filled with references to the institution of slavery. Slaves were a part of the culture of biblical times. How, then, can one speak of a religious commitment to the dignity of labor?

One need look no further than the twenty-fifth chapter of the Book of Leviticus to see the institution of slavery described, with all its discrepancies. Ancient Hebrews were not allowed to keep fellow Hebrews in bondage, but those who were not of the community could be enslaved permanently:

> And if thy brother be waxen poor with thee
> and sell himself unto thee
> thou shalt not make him to serve as a bondservant.
> As a hired servant, and as a settler, he shall be with thee;
> he shall serve with thee unto the year of the jubilee
> then shall he go out from thee, he and his children with
>   him
> and shall return unto his own family
> and unto the possession of his fathers shall he return. . . .
> Of the children of the strangers that do sojourn among
>   you
> of them may you buy and of their families that are with
>   you,
> which they have begotten in your land;
> and they may be your possession.
> And ye may make them an inheritance for your children
>   after you,
> to hold for a possession;
> of them may ye take your bondmen for ever.
>
> *Lev. 25:39–46*

Slavery was known throughout the ancient world for thousands of years before biblical times. It was a fact of life, an accepted part of society. Early biblical law did not try to eradicate such a long-established institution, but it did seek to humanize it. The twenty-first chapter of the Book of Exodus exemplifies that effort. Hebrew slaves were to be set free after seven years of service. If a female slave was "unpleasing" to her master, he had to let her be redeemed and could not sell her to outsiders. In biblical times, the master of a household could incorporate a female slave into his larger household, and she could and usually would bear him children. If he married another woman, he was obligated to provide the rejected female slave with food, clothing, and access to conjugal rights with another in the household. If he failed in any of these three ways, she was to go free.

An escaped slave was not to be returned to his or her master. In postbiblical times, when Jews were frequently enslaved by the Greeks and Romans, it was considered an obligation to redeem Jewish captives, usually by paying large ransoms. A people who had themselves been slaves in Egypt could never quite forget what it meant to live without freedom. "For you were servants in the land of Egypt" is a phrase that is laced through Jewish liturgy, history, and ethical admonitions. Later, particularly as Jews migrated to America at the turn of the twentieth century, the elimination of conditions of economic slavery — workers tied to their benches, their looms, and their sewing machines — became an issue that attracted major Jewish involvement.

Nowhere in the Bible can one find a reasoned defense of slavery. If the ancient Hebrews and the Jews of the early centuries accepted the institution, even as they tried to mollify its harsh conditions, the Greeks and Romans sought to justify it. Not only were their economic systems and lifestyles founded on and dependent on slavery, but slavery also became a philosophical tenet of their social and political outlooks. In *Politics*, Aristotle wrote a ringing defense: "From the hour of their birth, some are marked out for subjection, and others for command." He who can work only with his body is by nature a slave. "The slave is to the master what the body is to the mind, and as the body should be subject to the mind," so it is better for all inferiors that they should be under the rule of a master. The slave is a tool with life in it; the tool is a lifeless slave.

Aristotle's writing clearly reflects Greek, and later Roman, disdain for manual work. Aristotle saw it as something necessary, void of value, and fit only for slaves. He believed that manual labor dulled the mind, causing it to deteriorate and leaving neither time nor energy for political intelligence. Therefore he believed that only persons of leisure should have a voice in government. At Thebes, there was a law that no man could hold office who had not retired from business ten years before. Aristotle considered merchants and financiers to be in the same category as slaves. Moneymaking was considered unworthy of a free man. Aristotle and Plato may have differed on other philosophical matters, but they shared a remarkably similar view of slavery. Slaves were merely creatures made for work, to maintain the material well-being of the state. What became of them as human beings was to both men a matter of very little interest. They were simply a disposable commodity, much the way we would think of an obsolete toy or used clothing today. Some Greek schools of thought, notably the Sophists, had at least theoretical objections to slavery, but their views carried little weight.

At this time, one Jewish philosopher, Philo Judaeus, a resident of Alexandria during the first century of the Common Era (C.E. — after the birth of Christ), strongly disagreed with the prevalent Greco-Roman view of slavery. Influenced by his own Judaic background, Philo claimed that "servants are free by nature, no man being naturally a slave" (*The Torah: A Modern*

Commentary, 1981). In this he expressed the Jewish attitude of his day. The contrast between Judaism and the dominant sociopolitical system in which it existed and struggled to survive could not have been more stark. According to the Jewish view, even slaves were human beings with rights, not the least of them being the right to rest.

REST FOR WHAT PURPOSE?

Both versions of the Ten Commandments grant the slave the right to rest on the Sabbath together with his master. Exodus associates this right with the fact that even God rested on the seventh day (Exod. 20:9), while Deuteronomy pins the justification to the recollection that the Hebrews were once slaves (Deut. 5:15), a condition from which God liberated them.

The centrality and importance of Sabbath rest in Judaism cannot be too strongly emphasized. It is perhaps Judaism's most original contribution to world law. We do not know where the concept originated. Some scholars seek to tie it to earlier Babylonian practices. Others see the Sabbath as originating with the people of Israel in the desert wilderness during their sojourn there after fleeing Egypt. Most probably, the day was known to the Jewish people in their pre-Canaanite history, long before they established their first nation-state in the land of Israel.

The genius of the Sabbath is that it separates rest from labor, and by elevating one, it brings importance to the other. The accompanying ritual practices give it a divine sanction and thus ensure its permanence. We are not *asked* to rest one day a week; we are *commanded* to do so. We are to do it regularly, beginning each Friday evening. The fact that the Sabbath recurs every seven days, regardless of season or cycles of sun or stars, exalts God over time and nature. Once a week, we are asked to set time aside, to cease physical labor and likewise to cause our animals to cease their work. We are asked to do this not because labor is onerous or demeaning, but because labor is of such importance that one and all need to regain their strength through rest and to return to work refreshed and reinvigorated. The rabbis point to the words in Exodus: "Six days you shall labor" (Exod. 20:9). This, they say, is a positive command. With labor, human beings would emulate God's creative process.

Labor is or should be as dignifying as it is rewarding. How different is this approach from that of the Greeks and Romans. Here the sanctity of life is elevated and revered. Human beings are not machines to be used and used endlessly until they stop and then to be discarded. Human beings are not to be abused without concern for their welfare. The Talmud speaks repeatedly of the dignity of free labor. In Talmudic days, every rabbinic teacher had an outside profession or skill at which he worked — shoemaker, tailor, baker, woodcutter, night watchman, even grave digger. Every parent was commanded to teach his child a craft or trade. Work was seen as a virtue, not a curse; as a privilege, not a burden; as an opportunity, not a drudgery. Rest, the restorative medicine necessary to make it possible to continue work, creative or not, was sanctified. It was called the Sabbath, and it has become part and parcel of nearly every religion on earth.

In Islam, the Sabbath is called *yom al-jum'ah* (day of assembly). It is observed on Friday, the day in Islamic tradition when creation was completed and Muhammad made his first entry into Mecca, but it is not a day of complete rest. In Christianity, in 325 C.E., after the Council of Nicaea, the Sabbath was moved to Sunday, the day Jesus was reported to have risen to his permanent abode. This was also seen as a way to separate even more completely Christianity from its Judaic origins. At first, the Christian Sabbath did not carry the demands for rest attached to the Jewish Sabbath. Only later, during the Middle Ages, did rest become a major part of Sunday observance. But the ordered rest did not seem to be accompanied by any recommendations as to how to find pleasure in the experience. Instead, restrictions abounded, resulting eventually in prohibitive blue laws, which regulated work, commerce, and amusements on Sundays.

Over the millennia, Sabbath observance has generated a protective cocoon of practices, encapsulating a variety of expressions: worship, study, and joys, all designed to enhance the delight of Sabbath rest. The rabbis have even gone so far as to command that at least once a week, on the Sabbath, a couple must enjoy the pleasures of physical love. The twenty-four-hour period from sundown Friday to sundown Saturday is designated as a time for synagogue worship, family observances in the home, and rest for one and all. Mourning the dead is prohibited. Travel is restricted. The mood that is sought is one of serenity and reflection. The Sabbath is a time for spiritual as well as physical restoration, and it is not a time for painful restrictions.

For a long time, the Sabbath was very effective. It was the glue that held the Jewish community together. The Talmud tells us, "More than Israel has kept the Sabbath, the Sabbath has kept Israel." That was true until modernity imposed its own demands. For many, perhaps most, Jews and non-Jews, the reality of contemporary life is far different from the idyllic situation described above — outside the isolation of the ghetto or away from the solitude of an agricultural community. By the end of the nineteenth century, political and social emancipation had placed Jews in the open competitive market. Intellectual enlightenment weakened emotional ties to

Jewish tradition and practice. Whether out of necessity or conviction, severe, nearly fatal compromises were made in Sabbath observance. Old practices eroded, and the need to earn a living caused many Jews to set aside prohibitions of work. Christians, too, were and still are faced with serious compromises of their own Sunday Sabbath commitments.

The last decade has produced some remarkable and unforeseen changes in this regard. Ironically, while we Americans are increasingly a workaholic people, more of us find that we have weekends with time to engage in activities that are not work related. To be sure, these moments may be crowded with obligations for both children and adults, with long lists of unfinished projects, but unlike our parents or grandparents, most of us no longer have to open the store on Saturdays and maybe even Sundays, punch a time clock, or tend to the animals on a demanding and ongoing basis. Leisure time is now a precious asset in many of our lives.

Lifestyle changes allow us the luxury of exploring whether and how to take advantage of opportunities for rest. And some people, perhaps a growing minority, are reconsidering the role of synagogue or church worship as part of our new leisure time. Indeed, the celebration of rest through religious expression is being looked at by some as a source of joy. The Sabbath may be coming back into vogue, and while it need not and surely does not have a formal worship component for all, we might ask ourselves, "What will I do, or not do, today that I do, or do not do, on the other six days of the week to celebrate this day of rest and to refresh my soul?" Doing something outside, such as gardening, could be one response.

There has never been a better time to consider these options. People complain that they have no time, and many don't. Increasingly, I hear of or meet highly paid executives or talented men and women who turn down bigger salaries, and presumably better jobs that involve additional responsibilities and greater time commitments, because they want to do more than just work, because they want to spend more time with their families, because there is a world out there that they want to experience and have not yet had a chance to, or because they do not want to get stuck in a rut. I see people retiring earlier, and good for them. There needs to be a balance in life between work and rest. Maybe we are finally beginning to understand that and are seeking ways to achieve that balance. That is a goal prayerfully to be wished for.

There is a lovely rabbinic story. It was once asked of a rabbinic teacher, "When will the messiah come?" He replied, "When either every Jew in the world observes the Sabbath on the same Sabbath or when no Jew anywhere in the world chooses to observe the Sabbath anywhere in the world on any particular Sabbath. In the first instance, the world will deserve the messiah. In the second instance, the world will desperately need him." Nice story — maybe even true.

THE VALUE OF WORK

We do not ordinarily think of work in terms of nonmonetary value. Maybe that is because we do it so much. Surveys suggest that most Americans like to work and like their jobs. They like the discipline of work. They like the responsibilities and rewards, psychological as well as monetary, that accompany work.

In his magnificent novel *Heart of Darkness*, Joseph Conrad touches on this facet of work. Marlow, the protagonist of the story, is traveling up the Congo River on a fated journey to find Kurtz, a despotic ivory trader whom the natives fear and despise. Conrad describes the difficult work Marlow has to undertake as he pilots his craft up the amazing and treacherous river:

> It was a great comfort to turn . . . to my influential friend, the battered, twisted, ruined, tinpot steamboat. I clambered on board. She rang under my feet like an empty Huntley and Palmer biscuit tin kicked along a gutter; she was nothing so solid in make and rather less pretty in shape, but I had expended enough hard work on her to make me love her. No influential friend would have served me better. She had given me a chance to come out a bit — to find out what I could do. No, I don't like work. I had rather laze about and think of all the fine things that can be done. I don't like work — no man does — but I like what is in the work, the chance to find yourself. Your own reality — for yourself, not for others — what no other man can ever know. They can only see the mere show, and never can tell what it really means.

What is work's value? The challenge to find out who we are and what we can do and be. Work is an opportunity, a challenge to the creative self that lies hidden within each of us, waiting for us to uncover it. I know this truth: the work I have put into my garden has allowed me to uncover that inner self. When I first began, I had no idea what I could create — or if I could create anything at all. The garden evolved almost on its own. Whatever plan I may have had vanished as I cut some newly discovered curve in a garden bed or uncovered and moved a stone to a better place. I have often said that a plant will eventually tell you where it wants to go if you give it enough of a chance, and that is surely true. I moved a rose of Sharon bush three times until it finally found its proper place beside the steps leading from the pool to the deck above it. I moved a clematis twice until it finally found its spot next to the bird feeder, whose metal pole it climbs. It takes some plants longer to tell you than it takes others. Or maybe it takes me longer to hear them.

Work is important. Rest gives work dignity. The Sabbath gives it the insurance of sanctity. How many times have I said that I couldn't wait to get back to work? I think we all have said that at one point or another in our lives. I feel sorry for those who have not.

⁂

It has been a long journey down this garden path to my new bench. The bench is made of teak, and since it is still quite new, it has a lovely deep reddish cast. I guess I should oil it or put something on it to properly maintain it. I know about keeping teak bright. I once owned a forty-foot trawler, and she was replete with teak trim around all the ports and hatches, teak rails, and a totally teak deck. I can give lessons in teak maintenance. I took special delight in keeping up the teak on that boat — the pride that boat owners have in their craft. I have decided that my bench has too many ribs and legs with too many tiny, tough surfaces that I would constantly have to get into to keep the bench in its present hue. That would be too much work, so I will allow it to gray naturally. It will have its own natural beauty.

This has been a difficult chapter to write. I had to leave out as much as I included, and the decisions were exhausting. I am tired. Time to sit down for a while. My garden bench awaits my visit. Such a lovely view of the garden from there. And there is room for one more beside me.

CHAPTER IX

Poison Ivy, Healing, and Spirituality

He who saves one life is regarded as if he saved the world. He who destroys one life is regarded as if he destroyed the world.

Rabbinic teaching

P oison ivy is the bane of most gardeners. I got it a lot when I started to carve out the space that was eventually to become my first landscaped area. The area was a gardener's nightmare, hardly fit for the handwork method to which, in the absence of other mechanical devices, I was reduced. Bittersweet, planted initially by sportsmen as cover for pheasant they wanted to attract for shooting, had taken over and grew in rich, thick abundance. Bull thorn, a devastatingly tough and aptly named vine with extremely sharp thorns and a root system that runs not only horizontally just below the surface but also vertically to at least China, intermixed with the other vines and defied pulling, even as it resisted the normal chop strokes of the shovel. The pheasant were, of course, long gone from the area, but the weeds and vines continued to challenge me to eradicate them. Moreover, poison ivy had insinuated itself into the underbrush, where, untouched for years, it had become a thickness defying one and all. Concentrating, as I had to, on the heavier stuff, I ignored the poison ivy. It did not ignore me.

I remember the day of its attack as though it were yesterday. It was a hot, sticky, humid August afternoon — one of those days too hot for long pants or a sleeved shirt. Shorts, a T-shirt, and garden boots were about all I could tolerate. I had just filled the garden cart with armloads of stuff I had pulled out of the area and was dragging the cart up the drive to the compost pile at the back of the garden when I began to itch. Within an hour, the itch turned to massive red welts up my arms and down my legs. Even the back of my neck became a source of maddening irritation. Hivelike eruptions soon followed. My medicine cabinet was filled with highly touted "cures" for poison ivy: calamine lotion, Epsom salts, pills, lotions, you name it. I swallowed, smeared, applied poultices. Nothing worked, and I resigned myself to waiting; when poison ivy strikes, tough it out. And then I spotted the aloe vera.

The medicinal uses of aloe vera were well known to the ancient Greeks, and even before that time its healing powers were recorded in the literature of ancient Egypt. We kept an aloe vera plant around because we did a lot of cooking, and inevitably someone would get burned by hot grease or boiling water. We knew that when such an accident occurred, we could reach for the aloe vera, pull off one of the long green spikes, slit the spike open with a fingernail, and then smear the cool, clear, colorless gel on the burn. Presto, the pain would disappear, and shortly thereafter, any blisters would dissolve and the burn would begin to heal. In a day or two, it would be gone. Magic — yes, four-thousand-year-old magic.

I looked at the plant on the back porch, and a dim light went on inside my head. *Why not?* I thought. *It works for burns, sunburn included, and this stuff really burns right now, so why not?* I broke off a long spike, slit it open, and rubbed the gel onto one of my inflamed arms. Instantly, the itch stopped. In short order, every affected part of my body was covered with aloe gel. Within an hour, the welts disappeared. Within three hours, I did not even remember having had poison ivy. Bingo! I had made the greatest discovery since my ancestors invented rye bread. I have never worried about poison ivy since. I still get it from time to time, but the aloe plant is always handy. In the winter, I move it inside to the kitchen, water it once in a while, and let it be.

I have a friend who is a leading chemist for one of the nation's major cosmetics companies. I once asked her, "Why don't you emulsify aloe vera and market it?" (I actually once tried putting a bunch of the spikes in a blender with some mineral oil. The resulting goo lasted about a week before the stench overpowered even my insensitive olfactory capacities.) Her response was most instructive. It seems that all cosmetics companies know my secret. But were their products to contain more than 10 percent of the plant extract, they would have to label them as pharmaceuticals and not cosmetics, and that would radically alter their patents. What they currently sell may do some good, but I prefer my own concoction — 100 percent gel, nothing added.

PLANTS FOR HEALING

Using plants for healing is an ancient art, and aloe vera is only one of many plants with such powers. Most of us who garden probably have some medicinal plants in our growing spaces without even knowing their potential. Foxglove, one of our favorites, is a dramatic spring perennial that blooms biennially. To have a permanent bed of it, you need to plant it in successive fall batches. Its flowers, clustered close together, bloom all the way up the tall stem, and they come in a variety of colors, their appearance like a bright cluster of hanging bells. The scientific name for foxglove is *Digitalis*. Extracted and properly prepared, it has been used for hundreds of years to treat heart problems.

Echinacea is another common and very popular flower associated with healing — in this instance, the prevention of the common cold. Best known as coneflower, it is a lovely, daisylike plant with tall stalks and purple or white flowers. Lots of people buy echinacea in pill form at health food stores and take it on a regular basis. Does it work? Personally, I just put that plant in the ground. I prefer cultivating it for its beauty rather than its medicinal value.

Some plants are downright dangerous to our health. My garden has a large patch of aconitum (monkshood). Its flowers are almost royal blue, and when in bloom atop four- to five-foot stems, they make a dramatic counterpoint to the yellows that surround them. But I have been warned by nurserymen and others not to taste the leaves of monkshood because they are poisonous. The same is true of oleander, a large shrub that I cannot cultivate in my northern garden but that grows profusely and wildly in southern climes. It is beautifully flowered . . . and deadly.

HEALING AS A RELIGIOUS MANDATE

Healing of the sick has always had a very high priority in every culture, and the medicinal value of plants and even certain animal parts has been linked to healing as far back as history informs us. Originally, the use of these natural medicines was restricted to religious authorities — priests, shamans, and the like — and was shrouded in mystery and ritual. The knowledge and skills needed to use the materials effectively added to the mystique of such persons. It also gave them the power to control the society in which they functioned. Such is still the case in many societies throughout the world.

The Greeks of antiquity brought the practice of medicine to a high art, identifying four universal elements — earth, air, fire, and water — and four bodily humors, or fluids — blood, phlegm, choler, and black bile. Healers would prescribe various herbs for maladies that might occur in each of these humors. But even before the Greeks, we find an enigmatic healing tale involving serpents in the twenty-first chapter of the Book of Numbers. As the story opens, the people are, as usual, complaining of the miserable condition of their lives in the desert. God, tiring of their whining, sends poisonous snakes among them, and the snakes kill many with their venomous bites. The people, admitting that they were wrong to complain about their desert life, plead with Moses to intervene to halt the attack. Moses' response is to create a bronze serpent that he erects on a standard so that anyone who has been bitten can look at it and be healed. This story raised difficulties for later Jewish sages, as it seemed to violate the Second Commandment, which forbids the making of graven images. Later scholars have wondered how the incident crept into the Bible and when. Tales of the healing influence of serpents may be found in other cultural traditions as well. For instance, Asclepius, the Greek god of medicine, appeared in the form of a serpent. Thus the modern symbol of the medical profession, the caduceus, features two entwined serpents.

It is not an exaggeration to suggest that since biblical days, there has been a love affair between Judaism and the practice of healing. Undoubtedly, since Jesus was raised and trained in this Jewish world, the portrayal of him as a healer can be linked to this much-honored association. Judaism has always considered the maintenance of a healthy body as important as that of a healthy soul. The most succinct formulation of this doctrine is found in the words of Moses Maimonides, a famous twelfth-century scholar and physician, who in his summary of the codes of Jewish law wrote, "One should aim to maintain physical health and vigor in order that his soul may be upright, in order to know God. Whoever follows this course will be continually serving God."

What is important here is the realization that while the earliest biblical writing always portrays God as a healer ("Heal me O God and I shall be healed," cried the prophet Jeremiah in chapter 17, verse 14), healing was not left solely in God's province. Healing the sick was considered a sacred human activity, a doctrine that did not go unchallenged. Does not sickness, like health, come from God? asked some of the rabbinical sages. And if so, is it not wrong to interfere in God's plans? Would not such activity seem to betray a lack of faith in God as healer? Only rabbis can ask such questions. But never mind. The answer was provided through a Talmudic tale that will resonate with any gardener who has ever held a pair of shears in his or her hand.

Rabbi Ishmael and Rabbi Akiba were once walking through the streets of Jerusalem. A sick person approached and asked for a remedy. An observer, overhearing the conversation, challenged the two: "God has sent sickness, and yet you are telling this man how to be cured! Are you not working against God's will?"

The rabbis responded, "What is your livelihood?"

"I tend vineyards in order to grow grapes for wine," he answered.

"Do you prune your vines?"

"Of course. If I did not, there would be no grapes the next year."

"But who created the vineyard?"

"The Holy One, Blessed be He."

"Then do you not interfere with the vineyard that is not yours?" The questioner was silent for a moment, and the rabbis continued. "Just as the vines, if not cared for, will not produce their fruit, so with the human body. If not cared for, it too will not produce that for which it was created."

The view of illness here is instructive. Even if seen as a result of some unrighteous behavior, as stated in the twenty-eighth chapter of Deuteronomy, illness is curable as long as the person afflicted follows a specified regimen of atonement: prayers beseeching forgiveness and requesting healing; the use of folk medicines, usually swallowing some potion (see chapter 5 of Numbers for a description of the way a woman suspected of adultery was forced to drink bitter "water of contention" to bring out the truth); and finally the expression of thanksgiving for restored health and ritual purity. In short, sickness is not a permanent punishment for wrongdoing.

By postbiblical times, healing had become a recognized and required practice. The Talmud, Judaism's most complete and definitive source of binding law, written between the first and fifth centuries C.E., contains a lengthy section on home remedies in one of its tractates, called Gittin (67a–70b). Judaism teaches that humans are mandated to heal, and the sages resort to the interpretation of biblical text to irrevocably drive home the point. In the Book of Deuteronomy, we read the command to restore lost objects: "If you chance upon an object lost by your brother, you must restore it to him" (Deut. 22:2). The Talmud expands the meaning of this text to include rescuing a neighbor from danger, such as drowning or being attacked by an animal, to restore his body as well as his belongings. Maimonides saw this passage as a mandate to heal medically — to come to the aid of one who has lost his health and is in need of restoration.

Thus Judaism has long esteemed physicians and recognized their necessity. In fact, in one rabbinic tract, we find an admonition against living in a community where there is no doctor. By the late Middle Ages, medicine was the second most popular profession among the Jews of Europe. It was not unusual to find Jewish doctors ministering to popes, kings, and Christian nobility. That commitment has never diminished. Medicine remains a highly popular career choice among Jews, and while Jewish organizations no longer build hospitals as they once did in this country, those that do exist continue to serve the communities in which they are located.

THE LAYPERSON AS HEALER

Judaism has never restricted healing to members of the medical profession. Ordinary people are not only expected but are in fact commanded to visit the sick. It's considered a mitzvah, a divinely commanded obligation. This is only one of some 613 mitzvoth (don't ask how we got them all), but the command to visit the sick ranks very high on that list. The first-century rabbinic sage Rabbi Akiba warned, "He who does not visit the sick is like a shedder of blood." Strong language. Visiting, connecting to, and communicating with an ill person is emphasized because it is believed to contribute to healing, and there is no doubt that it does. Illness isolates, and people who are confined for long periods of time have a tendency to turn inward, focusing more and more on themselves and their physical problems. The external stimulus that comes from a person walking into a sickroom, be it in the home or in a hospital, can redirect the focus, bringing new insight, hope, and reassurance. As a rabbi, I can testify that visiting the sick is more than a social courtesy; it is therapeutic. It is good for both the patient and the visitor. I have never left a bedside without feeling better for having made the visit, no matter how desperately ill the person with whom I have been.

One of Judaism's religious tractates, called the *Shulhan Arukh*, has rules for visiting a sick person: one must not sit on the bed, one must not visit during the first three hours of the day, and so forth. Reading those rules reminds me of my personal rules of thumb, fashioned over the years. The first is to have an upbeat story or joke in mind, so that if the opportunity presents itself, I can share the story and bring a smile to the patient. Laughter is great therapy. For example: "Doctor, you must tell me, will anything help me?" asked a sick woman, well advanced in her years. "I'm sorry," the young doctor replied, "nothing I can do for you can make you any younger." The woman, in shock, said, "Younger? That's not my problem; I want to be able to get older." When Norman Cousins, the distinguished editor of the now defunct literary magazine the *Saturday Review of Literature*, developed cancer, he found a way to laugh for at least twenty minutes a day, whether by viewing a comic film, reading some jokes, or having a friend visit and tell him stories.

My second rule is to move the conversation to the patient as quickly as possible. If the patient feels like telling me something, he or she will. I just have to have patience and listen.

My next rule is to remember that unburdening is a part of the psychic healing process. Not all healing applies to the physical; sometimes it involves psychological completeness. I well remember visiting a hundred-year-old woman with a pin in her hip and a painfully broken toe suffered as a result of a fall. One night, as I sat with her quietly, she turned to me and said, "Rabbi, it's enough already. Kiss me good-bye. Tonight I die." I did, and she did. An example of healing? Yes. Her life was complete; she felt "healed."

Finally, I don't exhaust the patient by staying too long. Instead, I make successive visits. The more times I am with the patient, the closer the friendship, the deeper the intimacy, and the more helpful I can be. I always remember that the world looks different to someone lying in a hospital bed than it does to one standing beside it. It looks very different to one sitting in a wheelchair than it does to one pushing the chair. I learned that the hard way. While working on this book, I underwent a medical procedure called an angioplasty, which required an overnight stay in the hospital. Suddenly, my whole world took on a different shape. How grateful I was for my companion's presence, and how much I looked forward to attention from the nursing staff and my cardiologist. Their reassurances bolstered my spirits beyond any measure I thought possible.

Pastoral caregivers and families of those seriously ill know that sometimes lives and relationships are healed even when there is no possibility of a physical cure. In fact, serious illness often motivates people to seek a healing of the spirit by reestablishing relationships with estranged family members and friends.

Recognizing the value of visiting in the healing process, many religious institutions have groups in the congregation who commit themselves to visiting sick members. Known within my faith community as *bikkur cholim* groups, they date back to medieval times and functioned in eastern European communities up to the time of World War II. Communities have always developed their own health care systems to ensure that the sick are not left alone, unattended, or forgotten. But perhaps it is even more important today, in our vast, increasingly anonymous societies. We need to feel that someone cares for us, that the sensitivity of caring is still alive in a world where millions die unattended and ignored.

I buried an HIV-positive congregant, and the experience nearly broke my heart. Lester had become part of an HIV support group for Jewish men. During the last stages of his illness, when he had become bedridden, members of the congregation formed a special "visit the sick" group that bolstered him enormously in his difficult last weeks. At his funeral, one of the group spoke: "We all became a fellowship, his family. His death, like his life, bound us together more closely than we could have ever dreamed. Lester was our bond of life." That group became a permanent part of the congregation's committee structure (though we did not call it a committee), and the members developed real expertise as caregivers.

Congregations also create public liturgies where worshipers can pray for the recovery of family members or friends. The recitation of a prayer for one absent from the congregation because of illness is part of the regular Jewish worship service; it is called the Mi Sheberach prayer and is recited prior to the reading of the Torah. Worshipers are encouraged to call out the names of those for whom they wish the congregation to pray. In some congregations, people gather together at the front of the altar for the prayer, which seeks healing of the body and the spirit.

Nowadays, the socialization of caring goes beyond religious institutions, as hospitals are beginning to see the therapeutic possibilities in nonmedical healing practices. Clergy trained in healing skills work with doctors in hospitals. They do not seek to preempt the role of the physicians, as they recognize the difference between curing and healing. Curing uses medical procedures and practices; healing does not. Healing is a result. But the effect of healing may be facilitated by nonmedical procedures performed by caregivers trained in those skills. At least medical people are beginning to think so, and it has made a difference in hospital life.

One of the criticisms leveled against the medical profession is that it has become too mechanical, too uncaring, and that doctors have become nothing more than highly skilled practitioners. Sensitive to these criticisms, some doctors are now seeking to self-correct, to humanize the practice of medicine. One such effort is the Arnold P. Gold Foundation, established by Dr. Arnold Gold and his wife, Sandra. One of the country's most distinguished pediatric neurologists, Dr. Gold epitomizes, in both his professional and his personal life, the compassionate care that the foundation seeks to encourage. More than 140 medical schools now use some of the teaching methods developed by this foundation.

SOCIAL HEALING

Healing is such a personal experience that we sometimes forget its societal dimension. Although many individuals are ill and in need of healing, society also is in desperate need of ongoing repair. The effort to bring to society the same loving concern one brings to individuals is called in the Jewish tradition *tikkun ha olam*, "the repair of the world." Like so much else in our culture, it seems to have found its initial expression in the Bible.

By the tenth century before Christ, the ancient Hebrew community was no longer a group of nomadic tribes wandering from Canaan to Egypt through the Sinai desert and back again to Canaan. Instead, it had become a settled nation, with a shrine capital in Jerusalem, military enemies on all sides, and a sophisticated economy, with all its attendant values and ills. One does not need to be a serious student of ancient Palestinian life to be aware of the nation's excesses — vast disparities in wealth between rich and poor, dishonest business practices, personal moral laxity, marital infidelity; you name it, and the Israelites seemed to have had it. The prophets of Israel cataloged these transgressions: "Your very rulers are rebels. . . . Every one of them loves a bribe and itches for a gift; they do not give the orphan his rights and the widow's cause never comes before them" (Isa. 1:23). If Isaiah was harsh, the words of Amos seared: "They sell the innocent for silver and the destitute for a pair of shoes. They grind the heads of the poor into the earth and thrust the humble out of their way. Father and son resort to the same girl, to the profanation of my holy name. Men lie down beside every altar on garments seized in pledge" (Amos 2:6–8). Dire consequences were to follow.

The ills of Israeli society are also described earlier, in the nineteenth chapter of the Book of Leviticus, a document written well before prophetic times. It is here that we find clearly articulated the rules for proper social behavior. One is not allowed to curse the deaf or put a stumbling block before a blind person. One is prohibited from falsifying weights and measures. The gleanings of a field and the unpicked residue of a vineyard are to be left for the poor. One is commanded to pay his hired help at the end of the working day. The people are commanded to treat the alien in their land with the same laws of justice with which they deal with the native born. Finally, in a moment of grand hope, they are ordered to love their neighbors with the same passion with which they love themselves.

Surely, this is in every way a remarkable compilation of sacred social demands. No society since its enunciation more than thirty-five hundred years ago has ever come close to fulfilling it. No wonder there is a need still to find ways to repair the world. The major religions of the Western world take the mandate seriously and in their own ways strive to fulfill it. Every day, people young and old say to me, "Rabbi, I am not religious but . . . I volunteer at the soup kitchen because it is the Christian thing to do." Or "I am involved in this environmental group because it is a mitzvah to protect our natural resources." Or "I tutor in an inner-city school because we are commanded to learn and to teach." Healing is about improving everyday life, and it is in our daily lives that we can and do find opportunities to encounter God. The Judaic scholar and philosopher Martin Buber (1878–1965) taught us that we do a mitzvah whenever we treat another as a "thou" rather than as an "it."

Can anyone do a mitzvah? Of course. What makes mitzvoth special? Only the fact that not enough people take upon themselves their doing. Does doing a mitzvah make one more holy? No, but it might make you feel a little better about yourself.

THE DANGER OF SOME HEALING MOVEMENTS

Just as some plants are deadly when eaten, so are some so-called healing movements dangerous when entered into. Some groups and individuals promise those they can entice to join them not just enhanced self-esteem but also ultimate and eternal salvation. Many of these groups attract people who are looking for what our culture calls spirituality, a word and a concept that defies exact definition, something, I suppose, like trying to define love. Spirituality seems to be the religious buzzword of our age. At its best, it seems to me to be the pursuit of that which will bring a person inner tranquillity, connecting the person to what he or she sees as some ultimate wholeness, grounded inexplicably in eternal truth. This growing popular interest in finding one's own spiritual experience has boosted books on subjects such as the soul and near-death experiences to the best-seller lists.

While I am grateful that so many people today are searching for some deeper meaning in their lives, I confess that this focus on spirituality makes me somewhat nervous. As I write these lines, I cannot forget that the newspapers have reported how members of an Asian spirituality group publicly immolated themselves. Such tragedies both here and abroad are reported constantly. These may be extremes, yet increasingly we are seeing the emergence of groups that, in the name of spirituality, fellowship, brotherhood, or sometimes just plain hatred of others unlike themselves, express seriously damaging antisocial behavior. Spirituality — however defined and wherever found — must, it seems to me, be rooted not in negative beliefs, but in a positive personal and social goal.

Spirituality is sometimes linked today with what has been called New Age religion, a term that can conjure up a range of belief systems from astrology to Wicca covens. Perhaps the idea of spirituality has become whatever turns you on. A common question among people seeking spirituality seems to be, What is your practice? Putting the best light on such a query, it would translate as, What are you doing that will enhance your inner life? The answers seem to range widely from reading the Bible, to reading books about spirituality, to doing breathing exercises, to practicing yoga, to consulting the I Ching, to following a guru. The external practice, whatever it may be, is not to be judged on its own terms; the purpose is to bring about change in the inner state. Such changes seem to include achieving inner peace, a sense of well-being, and an expressed concern for others. One cannot always predict the inner effects of an external practice. In the context of health and healing, it is possible that inner resources may be found and developed to help a person bear pain, undergo trauma, or even face death with greater equanimity. It is easy to see how seeking and finding spirituality can have a strong relationship to healing.

JUDAISM'S RESPONSE TO SPIRITUALITY

Despite my reservations about spirituality as compared with what we in Judaism call the doing of mitzvoth, acts of social righteousness, I do recognize the connection between spirituality and healing the sick. I have spent too much time on hospice wards and have sat beside the beds of too many severely or terminally ill people. I know what prayer can mean and what it can do in such situations. Moreover, Judaism has a history of involvement with the quest for spirituality. Rabbi Jeffrey Salkin has observed, "Long before books about angels became a mega industry, Judaism taught (or rather sang) about angels" ("How to Be a Truly Spiritual Jew," *Reform Judaism* 24 [1995]). In fact, our Sabbath opens with a song of welcome to the ministering angels. And long before the dawn of the New Age, Judaism had developed rich traditions of mysticism and meditation. Even astrology is not foreign to the Jewish experience. In Israel, one can visit the remains of an ancient synagogue, in a place called Beit Alpha, whose floor is decorated with a large and magnificent zodiac.

Judaism actually began a serious flirtation with the mystical more than seven hundred years ago. A movement called Kabbalah, initially developed in Spain in the thirteenth century, reemerged in Palestine and the heart of the Byzantine Empire in the sixteenth and seventeenth centuries. Soon thereafter, however, it faded under the weight of the political emancipation and intellectual enlightenment that swept through Europe in the Napoleonic era. Kabbalah has recently enjoyed a renaissance among some spiritually oriented Jews, many of whom can be found in what is called the Jewish Renewal movement.

Judaism has accommodated all manner of approaches to the divine. Hasidism, a form of Jewish romanticism started in Poland in the eighteenth century, flourishes today in small pockets mostly in America and Israel. We have even seen and tolerated the arrival and departure of various proclaimed pseudomessiahs. Through it all, however, for mainstream Judaism, whether traditional or liberal, the doing of mitzvoth has remained the paradigm for expressing religious fidelity. The noted writer Cynthia Ozick has described this with straightforward clarity:

> The Jewish way is to be . . . responsible to your fellow creatures, not to be lifted above them by special intuitive or magical gifts of Divine apprehension; to express the Covenantal relationship by fellow-feeling in peoplehood, in duty, and in deed, not to make it secondary to subjective longings; to distinguish between the holy and the profane, not to wash away the holy by finding it everywhere in a great flood of undifferentiated and ubiquitous magical appearance; to attempt to control the self, not to follow the unyoked self's demand for equation with the forces of the universe.

THE INFLUENCE OF THE SHAKERS

We live near Hancock, Massachusetts, where one of our country's few remaining Shaker villages can still be found in pris-
tine condition. The community of Shakers are long gone,
their relatives scattered, but the buildings of their settlement
are maintained in excellent condition by a private group that
welcomes the many visitors who come throughout the year.
People come not only to see the famous round barn, the
dwellings, and the workshops, but also to watch the fields
being worked during the growing season as they were a century ago, by oxen pulling handheld plows. One of the most
delightful parts of any tour of the farm area is a leisurely visit
to the extensive herb garden. The Shakers were master
herbalists, and their extensive use of herbs for medicinal purposes is detailed in many of their journals. So famous were the
Shakers for their herbs that they were able to turn mail-order
sales into a lucrative business that significantly helped support
the community.

A fall visit to the Shaker farm is one of our family's annual
rituals, and of course we come away with great bags of herbs,
for which we spend far too much. I love it. But I have never
bought packets of herb seeds from the farm for spring planting. Why? Because I have never laid out or grown an herb garden. The absence of both space and full sun in my garden
have made such a venture too risky. But a change is upon us.

Last year, we decided to expand the house. If truth be
told, it was not we who made that decision; the children and
grandchildren did. Of course, we love their visits, but as the
grandkids grew from infancy to romping childhood, things
were getting a bit tight, and space needed to be found if for no
other reason than the continuation of familial tranquillity.

The builder, Michael, and his earth movers lumbered up our drive one day in the dead of winter. Later, I will describe his frontal attack on one of my most beloved and labored-over garden berms. (I am pleased to report that all that is behind me, and I have fully recovered.) For now, I'll note only that Michael's mighty machines turned out to be a blessing in disguise, especially the bulldozer. What a weapon that is. Old ash trees, whose girth measured at least twenty-four inches and that I had wanted down for years, tumbled like matchsticks before that monster's brutal blade. In one hour, I had before me at least a quarter of an acre of new, yearned-for space for my next, long-dreamed-of garden. (No gardener ever has enough space in which to work his or her imagination.)

As the equipment leveled the area, pulling out tree stumps, as it shuffled the newly created tree logs onto a flatbed and off the property, pale winter light poured onto the area. Suddenly, I realized my good fortune. The area the builder had cleared was in the southeast quadrant of our acreage, and southeast sunlight is, as any gardener knows, the best, most desired sunlight, since it is the warmest and the longest-lasting in a summer garden. A quick compass check assured me that spring and summer sun would drench the space.

Over the years, the woods and brush that had grown there had effectively blocked out the sun, causing me to think in terms of creating a shady woodland garden in a somewhat-cleared wooded area. Now my builder had inadvertently handed me a gift. It was as though I had dug up some treasure chest buried there ages past, filled with gold and waiting for me to discover it. Only this time, the gold was the sun's — far more precious to me than any base metal. The space and its possibilities boggled the mind. It was more than I could plot on my own. I placed a hurried call to a new young landscape architect whose work I had seen and whom I much admired. At our first meeting, we began to plan an herb garden, to be laid out in a geometric shape in a place both visible and accessible.

I do not expect to cure the world's ills with my home-grown herbs. I do not expect even to make one poultice for the first bee sting one of the grandchildren brings howling to me. But maybe, if I need a strong diuretic, I will make one out of the roots of a newly planted joe-pye weed (*Eupatorium purpureum*) or fashion a tea out of licorice, fennel, and lemon. They say that such a tea makes an excellent mouthwash and a refreshing cure-all. A tisane made from the leaves of English mallow soothes the throat, and those same leaves, crushed or pounded into a poultice, relieve aching muscles, bruised joints, and sprains. After I am through planting the garden I have in mind for my newfound treasure space, I am surely going to need that.

No, I will not cure the ills of society with my new herb garden, but I anticipate a healing of my own spirit — sometimes out of joint, sometimes angry with the world, sometimes at odds with myself. In his poem "The Road Not Taken," Robert Frost observes that "way leads on to way." Surely, I have found myself on a road that has led to a most unexpected clearing.

CHAPTER X

Letting Go

How Beautifully the Garden Dies

Do not go gentle into that good night,

.   .   .   .

Rage, rage against the dying of the light.

Dylan Thomas, "Do Not Go Gentle
Into That Good Night"

T he Berkshires are aflame in the fall. The sumacs are among the first trees to begin changing color and losing their leaves. Then come the sugar maples, the tall ashes, and the birches. Last to let go of their clothing are the majestic oaks. They hold their leaves, by now turned to burnt orange, into late October. What a magnificent spectacle. Fall in New England is legendary, and deservedly so. The reds, yellows, russets, and rich browns dazzle. Hiking, biking, or jogging around our lake with the pungent fragrance of dead and dying leaves filling my nostrils can intoxicate. I never want to go inside.

On a brilliant fall day, driving to Woods Whole, our Berkshire hideaway, can be breathtaking. I remember being nearly blinded once by the color of a huge sugar maple alongside the Taconic Parkway. The entire tree, a brilliance of gold, had not yet lost a leaf and seemed to have been set aflame by the afternoon sun. No wonder city dwellers flock to New England in the fall for weekends of viewing autumn foliage. It is a time when nature seems polished in amber and garnet hues. One wonders whether even a Cézanne, with all his artistic brilliance, could capture on canvas the natural beauty of that sight.

My companion once observed as we were kicking through a roadside pile of leaves, "How beautifully nature dies. Why can't we go out the same way — in a splash of color, falling toward death with no pain, no regrets, no fear, no complaining, knowing that what is happening to us is for the best, part of an important life-continuing plan?" That tells you something about her. As I look forward to spring, she anticipates fall. It's her season. She may not (yet) be great at picking up a rake to help with the fallen leaves, but her enthusiasm for the season makes up for her otherwise uncooperative attitude. She writes. I rake. A fair division of function, wouldn't you agree?

She has taught me to see fall in an entirely new way. Before, it was just a time to rake up leaves, cut down the garden's detritus, dig and store the dahlia tubers, lay in some spring bulbs, top-dress the beds, clean and put away the tools, and begin the long wait — for January and the arrival of the spring catalogs. Somehow, now, the season is different. Maybe it is because I am getting older and have entered the fall of my own life. Now I see that there is much beauty in a fall garden. Delicate, light violet colchicum (fall-blooming crocus) decorate the leading edges of one of my beds. (What a pleasant surprise, since I had forgotten I had planted them there last spring.) The asters make a brilliant (if leggy) purple, red, and white display, as do the mums. The dahlias are really in their element in early fall. They seem to explode in showy bloom: bright reds, deep oranges, delicate bicolor violet-and-white pastels — colors that seem to have been pulled from God's paint box. The phlox continue their tall, merry presence, while the anemones proliferate, much to the delight of the honeybees, who keep coming back for one last drink before heading home (wherever that may be). The burning bushes overwhelm their corner of the garden with their deep ruby–colored leaves on bushes of magenta-colored stalks.

Since the climate seems to be getting warmer, the display now lasts well into October; then things slowly begin to fade and die. How beautifully nature dies in the fall — so much grace, such elegance. To use an analogy, my garden in spring is like a beautiful adolescent — perky, a bit uncertain, but full of promise. By June, she has become a seductive young lady — cocky, sure of herself, and ready to show her fine young form. The summer months of July and August give me the delight one gathers from a mature, full-bodied woman, one who knows exactly who and what she is and who bestows pleasure with the joy of abundant giving. By the fall, she is older, perhaps a little matronly but still enormously charming, her sexuality muted but still seductive and captivating. There is life and love in her yet, and she knows it. She knows she is about to depart, but she will leave the stage only as a proud, magnificent star. As the winds of fall begin to muss the tresses of her plants, she seems to remember and rejoice in all her past incarnations. She knows the pleasure she brought, but it is time to go, and she is ready. She departs in a slow glide, with all her beauteous color in full display.

Why *can't* we live and die as nature does? A charming, but perhaps a bit simplistic, question. We can't live and die that way because although we are a part of nature, we possess faculties that the rest of nature seems to lack. The natural world I have just described cannot make conscious decisions. We can. Nature can only follow prescribed laws laid down eons ago; it cannot make conscious judgments to follow or ignore any one of those laws. We humans can, and we do, especially when it comes to life-and-death matters. Yes, eventually those natural laws do catch up with us — no living thing can avoid dying — but see how we struggle to avert the inevitable, to hold back death's cold hand as it reaches out to take ours. We make death-delaying decisions on a host of issues, and we create instruments of the most sophisticated kind to help us stay alive just a little longer.

Behold the ventilator. It does our breathing for us, even when we no longer can. Witness the wondrous mechanisms and medicines available to resuscitate us when we are at death's door. The arsenal is impressive: vaccines, insulin, laser beams, ultrasound scans, radiation, organ transplants, pacemakers, heart and lung machines. So ubiquitous are these instruments, so ready to be applied to our fading frames, that we or our loved ones have to anticipate their invasion by writing "do not resuscitate" (DNR) orders denying health care workers the right to introduce any life-preserving substance or instrument into or onto our bodies.

Not only can we decide whether to insert or pull the plug, thus continuing or ending life, but new techniques also have vastly expanded our options and our burden of having to make difficult ethical decisions regarding life and death. Perhaps the choices are sometimes too much and too many. Sometimes I think, *God, free me from my terrible choices. You decide who shall live and who shall die.* At one time, God did decide, or at least so it seemed. We lived and died according to forces over which we had no control, and people found solace in attributing what happened to God. Modern science has allowed us to take control of some, if not much, of that process. In a sense, we have co-opted what we thought was God's power. Today we often can decide who lives and who dies — or at least who may live a little longer.

Some plant lovers do the same things with their favorite houseplants. One woman I know, who happens also to be a nurse, once told me how she cared for her plants while she went on an extended vacation. She left the light on in her bathroom, placed the plants in her bathtub with the drain closed, and hung a large IV bag filled with water on a tall stand borrowed from her clinic. Through a series of plastic tubes, water slowly dripped onto her plants. The plants survived nicely, she told me, and some even put on a little growth. Ingenious, but childlike when compared to what we can now do to keep human life going a little while longer.

Sophisticated medical techniques create mind-bending ethical dilemmas that someone or some group has to solve every day. Hospitals now have medical ethics committees, called triage teams, to sort through the moral thickets and come to conclusions that are in essence life-and-death decisions. The following cases are hypothetical, but they illustrate the problems that many of us face on any given day.

A father has been diagnosed with terminal colon cancer. Should we provide him with hospice care so that he can die naturally under the watchful care of family and specially trained caregivers? Or should the doctor admit him to the hospital, where he will be put on life support, prolonging his death by an indeterminate number of days?

One sibling dying from a dread disease asks another, "Am I dying?" Should the healthy sibling tell the sick one the truth or finesse the answer?

A mother is now in her late eighties, in normal health but becoming very frail. If she stays in her home, where she has lived for the past half century and where she is totally comfortable, she is going to need nearly round-the-clock companionship. The cost for such care will exhaust the woman's resources in three months. On the other hand, if she divests herself of all her resources and hands them over to a private home for the elderly, to which she does not want to go, Medicaid will pay the bills, since she is now considered indigent. What should she do?

As our nation grays, care for our increasingly elderly population has grown from a simple cottage industry to a huge, highly lucrative business that will become even larger as science finds ways to enable us to live longer.

MAKING A LIFE-AND-DEATH DECISION

By the time my mother, Rebecca, was ninety-seven, she was deep in the grip of Alzheimer's disease. It had invaded her a decade earlier, but she seemed able to cope with it for a time. A widow for nearly a quarter century, she was fully active in the Jewish and general life of Cleveland, the community that she knew and that loved her so well. So widely known was she that her friends and colleagues would joke that they could sell "Rebecca dolls": "Wind one up and it will start an organization." She was like that. A whirlwind of knowledge, wisdom, and boundless energy.

At first, we did not know there was anything wrong. My sister lived in Boston, I in New York. Both of us were in regular phone contact with her, but she was able to mask her condition. It was not until her friends began to share with us revealing incidents of her illness that we knew it was time to move her to my sister's home. She lived there until she was nearly ninety-six and in need of round-the-clock care. So we moved her again, to the local Hebrew Home for the Aged. There, she had her own room, filled with memorabilia that in her moments of recognition seemed to bring her joy. As her memory and conscious awareness weakened, Mom was moved up to the floor that is called, in social work terminology, the Total Care Unit. In the words of a colleague, Rabbi Cary Kozberg, who serves as a pastoral counselor in such a unit,

> A Total Care Unit is a place where failing physical strength and diminishing mental capacity are acknowledged realities for residents, a place where the Angel of Death is ubiquitous and unrelenting — another world where the language is different, as are the rules of communication and socialization. Dementia brought on by advanced Alzheimer's disease, organic brain syndrome, or stroke have made cognition and the capacity to reason impossible for its citizens. In this place grunting, bleating, and even blank stares may substitute for normal speech; screaming and yelling may replace more familiar forms of articulation.

I visited Mom in the home as frequently as time and professional responsibilities allowed. (As she would remind me, it was never often enough.) And I began to see firsthand what Rabbi Kozberg has described: aged and frail human beings, living dead in their beds, sometimes in wheelchairs in the hallways, sometimes gathered together in a macabre sitting room, staring at nothing but one another, some screaming, some mumbling incoherently. The nurses would tell me that many

no longer had visits from anyone; these were people abandoned by their families, a fact the nurses could not comprehend. In some cases, the only familial contact was a check sent
monthly to the hospital's administration office. I have seen
this situation repeated many times. Would not these people,
living somewhere between death and life, be better off if they
were released from the torment of such a nonlife? How do we
decide when to stop prolonging life? No conference of oak
trees ever raised that question.

The query became real when our mother developed
pneumonia. Staff physicians, social workers, and ethicists
gathered with my sister, her husband, and me. In the absence
of any ethical will previously written by our mother, and without prior written instructions from her regarding whether or
not to take "heroic measures" to keep her alive, a DNR decision had to be made. Tears flowed. An emotional brew of
sorrow, guilt, and anger broke through, but finally the decision was made. Mom was ninety-seven. She had lived a full
and productive life. She was really out of it. It was time to
let go, say good-bye, and leave. We decided to let nature take
its course. Drugs to control discomfort or pain would be
administered, but under no circumstances was our mother
to be placed on any kind of life-support system. The pneumonia deepened, and Mother went into a comatose twilight
zone. Two days later, she died in her sleep quietly, painlessly.
How do we know she felt no pain? The doctors reassured us,
but I like better the reassurance I had earlier discovered in
Lewis Thomas's wonderfully rich small volume *The Medusa and
the Snail.*

Reflecting on the death of a mouse, the victim of his
house cat's natural proclivity, while simultaneously remember-
ing the loss of one of the large old elms on his property,

Thomas observed, "The main difference, if there is one, would be in the matter of pain. I do not believe an elm tree has pain receptors, and even so, the blight (which killed the tree) seems to me to be a relatively painless way to go even if there were nerve endings in a tree, which there are not." About the mouse and its dying, he continued:

> At the moment of being trapped and penetrated by (the cat's) teeth, peptide hormones are released by cells in the hypothalamus and the pituitary gland; instantly these substances, called endorphins, are attached to the surfaces of other cells responsible for pain perceptions; the hormones have the pharmacologic properties of opium; there is no pain. . . . If the mouse could shrug, he'd shrug. . . . When it is an end game, and no way back, pain is likely to be turned off, and the mechanisms for this are wonderfully precise and quick. If I had to design an ecosystem in which creatures had to live off each other and in which dying was an indispensable part of living, I could not think of a better way to manage.

PAIN AND SUFFERING

There is a difference between pain and suffering. Pain is physical and can be managed physically. Most hospitals today have pain management specialists on their staffs. Suffering, on the other hand, is psychological, and it even has sociological and theological implications. Herein lies an interesting bit of history. But before entering into that thicket, let us be clear that Judaism believes that pain should be managed — that is, contained, if not eliminated — because it sees no underlying virtue in pain.

In Judaism, pain is not seen as some independent good, inflicted on us by a divine power in order to either test our faith or cleanse us of some error in our ways. Pain provides no benefit, and since we view medicine as a practice designed to benefit the person — to improve the person's physical condition — the administration of medicines that will do that not only is permitted but is mandated. Painkilling drugs such as morphine may be administered to reduce pain when the illness is not fatal, and they certainly should be used to reduce pain in cases where the person is dying. If the pain is intense, a sufficient dosage may be administered to dull the pain, even if this simultaneously hastens the person's death. The intent to treat is the crucial factor. A caveat is obvious: no doctor can deliberately give a terminally ill or dying person a massive shot of morphine to "take him out of his or her pain." But doctors have been known to do that. Are they murderers? There are some who believe that life, even if it is excruciatingly painful and without any prospect of improving, is better than no life. I am not one of those. If I believe that it is morally and religiously justifiable to withdraw life-support systems from the terminally ill, then surely I must believe that it is justifiable to help reduce unbearable pain, even to the point of risking the hastening of death.

Most religions find theological justification for the alleviation of pain. Suffering, however, has a different history and evokes a different response. There are religious traditions that even today view the acceptance of suffering as a positive value. And they find biblical precedent for their position: "Blessed is the man upon whom You place sufferings" (Ps. 94:12).

I was surprised to learn that even my own tradition contains the following: "Bodily suffering is a suffering of love, if it is not sufficient to make a man neglect Torah and prayer. Such sufferings are sufferings of love, for they purge all the iniquities of man. As the salt cleanses meat, so chastisements purify the sins of man" (Talmud Berachot 5a).

In the history of religion, suffering has been accepted as an integral part of the process of repentance, an essential ingredient for the purification of the soul. But why? Why would anyone or any group make a virtue out of suffering? The answer is obvious: accept what you cannot change and transform a negative into a positive, thus giving its presence some meaning. This understanding developed at a time when neither physical pain nor suffering, both physical and social, could be alleviated or eliminated. Until less than a century ago, the simplest of maladies could kill you. An abscessed tooth, gout, leprosy, asthma, frostbite, tuberculosis, measles, poverty, even pregnancy, could and did bring enormous and unrelievable physical pain. Persecution and ethnic and racial hatreds caused social suffering. A rationale had to be found to justify the presence of such suffering, and it was: God's will. Therefore, learn to tolerate and accept suffering, with the hope (for some, promise) that you will be rewarded (recompensed) in the next world for tolerating here what would otherwise be intolerable. "The righteous, though they suffer (perhaps *because* they suffer), shall inherit the world to come" became a common religious theme. Suffering was thus transformed into a positive good. For some, it was welcome. During the Middle Ages, for example, people practiced self-flagellation for the sake of God.

There were consequences to such an attitude. Because suffering was seen as a means to a greater good, it could not be used to justify ending life. Thus euthanasia or anything that smacked of it was prohibited and was branded as murder, plain and simple. Theologians reasoned that to end life in ways other than through some noble war was to endanger, if not destroy, the spiritual benefits that such suffering could bring to the one afflicted. Does such logic apply today? Hardly. I am not the least bit unhappy that I was not born into medieval times, ugly and brutish as they were.

I cannot get out of my mind the memory of that Total Care Unit and my colleague's all-too-accurate description of it. I cannot help thinking that such units are places where we are merely warehousing the barely living. Are we being fair to them, to their families? No one really wants to discuss the issue, but it must soon be faced, as these spaces are filling up fast as a result of improved medical technology.

It is painful to see a person die. It is also painful to see a plant you have nurtured die, but we understand that a plant has a natural life span, and we can let it go. Besides, a plant does not have what we call a soul. We like to believe that people do. So why can't we think that letting a person die is freeing a spirit? We do and we don't — the paradox of humanity.

We no longer accept pain as a given to be endured. Should we not allow individuals who are incurably ill and barely living the right to gain release through physician-assisted death? My own religion walks a fine line here. We teach that while it is forbidden to take a life, it is permissible not to interfere with dying. In practical terms, that means that while Judaism would not countenance the administration of a drug for the express purpose of killing someone, it does allow a DNR order to be issued that will by definition speed the death of a dying person. In Judaism, prolonging life is seen as a positive act; prolonging dying is not. A rabbinical sage of the thirteenth century, Rabbi Nissim of Gerondi, wrote, "It is permissible to stop the clattering noises or the pounding of the wood near the patient because the noise delays the soul's departure. It is permitted to remove an impediment to death." Judaism may be life intoxicated, but it is also very realistic.

THE CASE FOR EUTHANASIA

Society is slowly developing structures, legal and otherwise, that allow surrogates the right to make life-and-death decisions for those who, through age or illness, are incapable of making those decisions themselves. The two most famous cases that furthered this process were those of Nancy Cruzan and Karen Ann Quinlan. Their parents gained the right to remove heart and lung machines and feeding tubes from the girls, both of whom were comatose. While these actions hastened their deaths, in both instances the girls survived longer than anticipated when the machines were removed, making a tragic situation even more difficult.

Society will soon tackle the more difficult cases of what to do with people in a permanent vegetative state. Since these people are not in danger of imminent death, their continued existence raises the ethical question of whether their deaths should be hastened in any way. There are some who believe so. Using a quality-of-life argument, they would hold that humans are not meant to live like vegetables. To keep them alive in such a state compromises their humanity and does them and life itself an unacceptable disservice. Hitler carried the matter even further. Not only did he mandate the destruction of such people, but he also reasoned that people he considered inferior polluted the human race and should be put to death in order to improve humanity. This was an extreme interpretation of eugenics, the science that deals with the improvement of the human race by selective breeding.

I do not make the case for eugenics or its modification, physician-assisted suicide. As a Jew, I know its dangers and its terrible consequences. Six million Jews died in Europe during the Holocaust because a madman believed, and persuaded the majority of his countrymen to accept the idea, that Gypsies, homosexuals, and Jews were in every way inferior and needed to be eliminated for the good of the German race and humankind. The Holocaust was the practice of eugenics run amok. It cannot be considered as anything even approaching euthanasia, since it could not even pretend to be motivated by any compassionate concern for humanity. The Holocaust was arbitrary, brutal mass murder. Plain, simple. Vile.

How, then, should I view the Dutch parliament's decision in the year 2000 to allow doctors to help end the lives of seriously ill patients who have asked to die? This decision, passed into Dutch law in April 2001, raises the question of euthanasia from a totally different perspective — the quality of life, not its insignificance. Historically, many nations have for one reason or another killed groups or classes of their own people. As a method of population control, ancient Sparta left female infants exposed to the elements to die. For the same reason, contemporary China promotes the abortion of female fetuses, a practice that even so strong an opponent of abortion as Pat Robertson unwittingly, and according to a later "clarification" inadvertently, endorsed in an interview on national television (see *New York Times*, April 18, 2001). But it was Nazi Germany that cruelly raised the practice to a brutal and abhorrent national policy. Between 1939 and 1941, the Nazis clandestinely murdered about 100,000 physically and mentally handicapped men, women, and children.

Of course, the new Dutch law has nothing in common with Nazi Germany's racist practices; it does not legalize a practice designed to eliminate an entire race or class of people. The Dutch have enacted the legislation because they consider the quality of life as valuable as life itself — a very sophisticated attitude. In the United States, only the state of Oregon has enacted similar legislation.

The Dutch law incorporates guidelines drawn up by the Royal Dutch Medical Association that carry strict stipulations: A patient's request must be voluntary and persistent, made while the person is lucid. The physician must be convinced that the patient is facing interminable and unbearable suffering. The doctor may not suggest death as an option. In all cases, physicians must seek a second opinion before helping a patient to die, and they must report the cause of death as euthanasia or suicide. Every doctor has the right to refuse if a patient asks for help in dying. The law does not apply to people under twelve, and terminally ill children from twelve to sixteen need parental consent.

The new law formalized what had become common practice in the Netherlands over many years. It is estimated that during the past decade, about thirty-five hundred people a year had died through this carefully prescribed procedure. In about 85 percent of the cases, the deaths occurred at home, usually through lethal and painless doses of barbiturates administered by family doctors — a procedure that is quite similar to the way most states in America "mercifully" execute their criminals.

According to an article in the *New York Times* (April 11, 2001), the Dutch law has evoked a firestorm of opposition, especially in Europe, with German clergy and media leading the attack. The Roman Catholic Church has denounced the new legislation as "a law that goes against human dignity." German doctors have denounced the practice, warning that "the dangers of abuse are too great." Surveys in Europe, however, reveal a difference between official views and public opinion. More than 80 percent of Dutch citizens support the law, and 64 percent of western Germans and 80 percent of eastern Germans feel that a critically ill patient should have the right to die. That this new law has such widespread support is of interest but cannot be the factor that determines either its correctness or its moral legitimacy. After all, the German people tolerated Hitler's destruction of Jews, homosexuals, and Gypsies.

Opponents of the legislation raise many troubling questions, not the least of which is their deeply felt concern that such legislation furthers a culture that continues to cheapen life. For whatever reasons — overpopulation, crowded living conditions, the economic burdens of keeping the old and the infirm alive — we seem to be in a hurry to get rid of those who are an inconvenience or a burden so as to make room for the new, the young, the healthy, and the potentially productive. Matters conspire to make life increasingly valueless, expendable, and laws like the one passed in the Netherlands merely contribute to this process. While we preach that life is sacred, we act as though it were worthless.

I hear this argument, but I respectfully disagree. The taking of life authorized by the Dutch law comes into being not because the Dutch care less about life than any other society and not because their culture holds life cheaply, but because they have been courageous enough to openly and honestly confront the flip side of the coin of life: its quality and the respect we need to show others who cherish that quality even more than they desire the continuation of life. Perhaps we are moving to a point in our philosophical outlook where the former weighs more heavily and is due more consideration than the latter.

It is nearly three decades since my daughter's tragic accident and death. Those who saw her fall from the horse she was riding testified that "she fell like a stone." She made no move to brace herself as she hit the ground. She was not wearing a helmet; in those days, that was not required. Her head hit a rock, which caused a massive subdural hematoma in the brain. Doctors told me that had she lived, she would have been a vegetable. Many times I have asked myself, "Is that what you would have wanted for Elisa?" Had I been at the hospital and had the physicians or staff asked me, would I have said, "Keep her alive at all costs"? As I look back over the years, I do not think I would have made such a decision. Elisa was too vital, too exuberant, too enamored of life to have wanted merely to exist. I believe I would have said, "Let God take her."

Understandably, this personal experience colors my response to the next question that emerges for me. Were I a rabbi practicing somewhere in the Netherlands, would I support or oppose the new legislation? I would end up in the support column, and since there has apparently been no outpouring of dissent from the Dutch clergy, I suspect that is where most of them also stand.

Can one make a case for physician-assisted death and the decriminalization of acts that bring merciful death to those who request it when, by any determinative standard, their quality of life has reached zero? I think so. Should a member of the clergy share information with those who ask about organizations such as the Hemlock Society and other recognized groups that provide help to people who wish to know more about how to best and most painlessly end their own lives? Judaism would say an emphatic "No!" We can take no action that might be perceived as hastening the death of another person, any more than we can take any action that might hasten our own deaths. Sharing information with another that might contribute to that person's death would violate that prohibition. Yet I confess that I have done so. Does it trouble me that I have broken with Jewish tradition? I see that tradition as a guide but not as an entity that totally governs my life. It is not my final moral arbiter. It is certainly an important component, but one of a number of critical factors that come into play as I struggle to make moral and ethical decisions. There are many ways to die.

THE HOSPICE ALTERNATIVE

A principle in the rabbinic tradition states that we need not try to cure a person who to our best knowledge cannot be cured. That is the initial justification for the hospice movement, a program based on the assumption that the person entering it is going to die sooner rather than later as a result of his or her illness, usually some form of cancer. Hospice does not seek to cure. It seeks only to help those who come under its umbrella to be as active and as free of pain as possible in their remaining days. It focuses on quality, not length, of life at its end. Unlike a hospital setting, where family members are often shoved off into waiting rooms, hospice asks loved ones to help provide essential care so that the dying person can remain at home and, if possible, die there in familiar surroundings and in the arms of family and friends. It does not hide death, or hide from it. Hospice involves every family member in death. It is honest care, open and realistic, and for some it is too difficult.

I once had a friend whose emotions I trust say to me through her tears, "I wouldn't want to burden my family. I want to spare them the agony of having to see me die and take care of me in the process." I understand that, even though I believe that she would be denying her family a profoundly important opportunity to say to her, "You are no burden. We love you. This, too, is what love entails." Perhaps she is transferring to them an as yet unresolved problem she has with her own love of her family. But, then, what do I know? I'm not a psychiatrist. I do know that hospice is a desirable and religiously acceptable form of care, and it is growing in popularity. There were 1,400 hospices and 158,000 hospice patients in 1985. A decade later, those numbers had grown to 3,000 hospices and 450,000 patients. Since people enter hospice programs with the full knowledge of their condition and its implications, there is no need to struggle with the question raised earlier about whether or not to tell someone the truth when the person asks if he or she is dying.

TRUTH TELLING AND THE TERMINALLY ILL

There isn't anyone in the religion business who has not been asked that question. Perhaps there has been some reasonable difference of opinion concerning the answer, but not since 1991. That year, Congress passed the Patient Self-Determination Act, which in effect gave all patients in the United States with full mental capacity the right to determine the course of their health care treatment. This made it nearly mandatory that patients receive adequate information from their physicians in order to weigh the benefits and burdens of proposed methods of treatment, including life-sustaining treatments, and either consent to or refuse those options. That legislation was a long time coming, and it has changed the way we deal with illness, especially terminal illness. We now know that dying patients do not fear death as much as they fear isolation, pain, physical deterioration, and being infantalized.

Withholding vital information has always been bad practice psychologically, despite the religiously held belief that giving patients such information could in some way shorten their lives. The fear was that patients would become despondent thinking that their physicians had abandoned them. My own movement of liberal Judaism was equally guilty of such foolish thinking. Some years ago, one of our rabbinic experts decided that it was clearly wrong to tell a patient that his or her case was hopeless and that he or she was dying. But in the past thirty years, study after study has indicated that patients want to know their diagnoses; such information seems to strengthen their resolve. Knowing what lies in the immediate future enables a patient to better plan for it. One physician specializing in prognosis, when asked whether being honest with patients poses the risk of removing their hope, wisely responded:

> The way out of that conundrum is to recast our vision of hope. We need to have hope and optimism not about the cure of the disease but about a variety of other objects so the object of our hope shifts at the end of life. We could be hopeful and optimistic that the patient will have an excellent quality of life. And we can be hopeful and optimistic that the patient will have excellent communication with relatives. Or we can have hope and optimism that patients will have excellent care, really wonderful care at the end of their life. . . . We can have hope and optimism that the patient will have a good

death. ("A Doctor with a Cause: What's My Prognosis?" *New York Times*, November 28, 2000)

A physician's withholding truthful information from his patient can dangerously weaken the trust between them, and once that is damaged, the patient may begin to question past or future information or treatment the doctor has provided. The same holds true for the relationship between clergy and patients. I remember once being asked by a dying congregant to participate in a conspiracy of silence, to join him in not telling his family of his imminent death. I refused, telling him, "Jerry, after you die, I'll still have to deal with your wife and children. You want to put me in the position of having to defend our lying to them? You'll be gone, so I'll get no support from you." We started to laugh so hard that tears came to our eyes.

A GOOD DEATH

Most of us would like to die like a leaf falling from a tree — in ripe old age, with no regrets, filled with radiant sagacity, gaily dancing down to a peaceful and painless end, surrounded in loving attendance by those who survive us. That would be a good death. But it does not always happen that way. Still, we can try to make it happen. To paraphrase a distinguished theologian, the late Rabbi Seymour Siegel of the Jewish Theological Seminary, we must not forget, in our loyalty to our traditions, religious or otherwise, the welfare of the suffering patient who, when the Giver of Life has proclaimed the end of his earthly existence, should be allowed to die in spite of our machines. Or, as Woody Allen is quoted as having once said, "I don't mind dying. I just don't want to be there when it happens."

I think about these things as I revel in the russets, reds, golds, and oranges of the trees along the highways and byways of my area. I think about these things as I rake leaves and find myself enriched by the fragrance of their death: no complaining, no suffering, no pain. Nature has lived meaningfully, and she dies easily, contentedly: no regrets. I think about that a lot. In the fall of my life, I, unlike the trees and plants, live with regrets. And who does not have regrets? For myself, I have been twice married and twice divorced, but now I am fortunate enough to have found a fulfilling life with a stimulating and creative companion.

Some people might ask how I can continue to be a clergyman, with such a poor marital track record. I understand that concern, but should the fact of divorce really exclude one from the rabbinate or ministry? Do people who answer that query in the affirmative think that those who have experienced the pain of divorce learn nothing from the experience and are not in some ways deepened and sobered by it? Do they think that we have learned nothing from the pain we have inflicted on others and felt ourselves, or that out of the fire of separation, we might not have learned something enabling us to be of help to others who may come to us when they experience a similar severing in their lives? I know the psychological and spiritual price one pays in reputation and the confidence of others when divorce is a part of one's curriculum vitae. There are some in my congregation who are deeply disappointed in me and angry at me, and who will never ask me to share in either their joys or their sorrows. That grieves me. More seem either not to care or to have put any disappointment behind them. Or perhaps they are so involved with their own lives that they cannot and do not give a tinker's damn about the details of mine. That is fine. I am here for them when they call, and I am happy to report that some still do.

Divorce is not one of life's more desirable experiences. I do not recommend it to anyone. It hurts, and it costs in more ways than just financially. But it is not the end of the world, and my faith allows for its happening. In Judaism, divorce is not a sin. It is the way we reconcile mistakes we have made and from which we cannot turn back. Judaism makes provisions for divorce, including the financial protection of the former wife. Divorce can, and usually does, knock one down, but it does not preclude one's finding a new way to make new beginnings.

I think about these things as I cut down the dead dahlia, aster, and helenium plant stalks in the garden, some still with flower heads blooming weakly on them. I think about these things as I drop hundreds of thumbnail-size crocus bulbs into their shallow winter beds. How beautifully nature dies in the fall, and what wonderful lessons it teaches us: when the time comes, we have to let go.

There is solace in watching the death of a garden. For therein lies hidden the assurance that in the spring, a mere few months away, it will return, and the same flowers will burst back into bloom. Is there not something for us to learn from all that?

Epilogue
Faith Comes Last

It is winter now, a good time to write an epilogue. Endings and winter dormancy somehow seem to go together. Both are good times for reflection, summing up. Now the snow lies deeply on the garden. We have a lot of it this year — a couple of feet on the ground. The bird feeders we keep full during the winter are getting a lot of action, and one nuthatch has commandeered the suet ball I made and hung on a straightened coat hanger right outside the sliding glass door in our living room. He can eat hanging upside down. He is a perfect combination of comic and acrobat.

Our house seems to be situated in some kind of snow pocket. Half a mile away it can be clear, or the snow cover a mere dusting, while our property is covered by three feet of the white stuff. It makes for a lot of shoveling and plowing, but I love it. Snow is not only a wonderful insulation for the plants; it is also a quiet blanket on the land. The stillness of a heavy snow covering allows me to think, to reflect. "The woods are lovely, dark and deep," wrote Robert Frost, who captured this spirit in his moving poem "Stopping by Woods on a Snowy Evening."

At times, the snow is too deep for me even to get out in the yard. No reason to check the pond to see if the goldfish and the shubunkin are all right. I know that they are not there. A great blue heron breakfasted on them one October morning. I caught him in the act, frightened him, and obviously interrupted his meal, for as he took off like a huge 747, one of my favorite and largest goldfish slipped from his grasp and fell to the ground. I buried it under a new magnolia I had planted that spring. Nothing goes to waste.

I look out at my sleeping garden and drift off a bit. Lord, the work that has gone into it, and still it is not right. I am going to have a backbreaking spring. As I mentioned earlier, we started an addition on the house this winter, and while bulldozing for the foundation, a workman unwittingly dumped the excavated earth on a large planted berm at the top of our drive. At least four feet of dirt now sit on top of a couple of hundred spring bulbs, some prize iris rhizomes, a few large decorative boulders I had dragged into place, and God knows what else. I practically went into cardiac arrest when I drove up the drive and got my first glimpse of that mess of mud. Now I know what it must feel like to have one's home caught in a flood or some other natural disaster.

Overwhelmed is a good word for starters. *Grief stricken* catches the full flavor of my initial reaction. The builder tells me that he saved those rocks, trees, and shrubs he saw by lifting them off to the side of the berm and placing them under a few bales of hay for protection, but I can't find them. Maybe they will show up this spring. If not, a lot of hard work lies permanently entombed. In addition, I have to move a couple of the tree peonies, resettle the big 'Blue Peter' rhody in a locale where its dramatic beauty can be better displayed, and enlarge the dahlia bed. The edges of the beds need more primrose plants for early-spring color. I wonder whether this year the clematis will finally make its appearance. What a struggle that plant has gone through. They say it takes three years; we'll see. Be patient — and stop crying.

FAITH COMES LAST

Gardening is a never-ending process. Gardening requires an act of faith, which sometimes justifies itself, but faith alone cannot a garden make. Faith is a fulfillment, not an initial motivation. If I do things right, the laws of nature will fulfill themselves, and my faith in those laws will be justified. If I ignore the rules, the Master Gardener sneers and turns away, and the plant dies. Faith comes at the end of the process. Faith comes last. Maybe that should have been the title of this book. The entire thrust of this volume is to help you understand that in order to construct a faith that will stand up to the rigorous challenges of our modern age — be they from science, cynicism, or despair — one needs a belief system that can sustain even the shattering blows of a Holocaust, a lying president, glib politicians, deceitful business leaders, sexually immoral clergy, dysfunctional adolescents, and unfaithful spouses. Maybe some people get through such moments and such times by relying on prayer or the guidance of their traditional faith or by throwing up their hands in ecstatic prayer, hoping that "God will save." But I think that even more of us just quietly walk away from "a God that failed."

This does not mean that many of us are not looking for something in which to believe. We are. The search for "spirituality" has never been more intense than it seems to be nowadays. The problem is that large numbers of highly educated and highly trained people are not finding solid answers to their doubts and questions in the structures of conventional religion. Religion has asked us to believe and accept so much that runs counter to our logical minds that we have learned to suspend our critical selves when we walk into a church or synagogue. Sometimes when we are there, we hear the words, but they do not even register in our brains. Since we do not expect too much that will stimulate us intellectually or spiritually, we numb out, dumb down, and enjoy the music.

That is a terrible situation. People should not have to stop thinking when they enter a religious institution. Such space ought to stimulate people's minds, not render them incomprehensive. Increasingly, I am persuaded that the beginning of all faith ought to be inquiry, doubt, and disbelief. Our first statement ought to be "I wonder," not "I believe." The first demand we make on our clergy or theologians ought to be "Show me! Convince me. Make what you teach here square with what I learn in the lab or the classroom or, for that matter, in the garden." If faith is to come (at) last, then surely doubt must come first. I hope that this volume has responded to some of those doubts and wonderings. I hope that I have bent some of the question marks into affirming exclamation points. I hope that I have been able to help you understand that faith is not a fixed phenomenon, not a body of answers, so much as it is a process, a constant refinement, a constant incorporating of new knowledge and new wisdom from many different sources.

Spirituality is a state of being, not a sudden ecstatic moment. It is the empathic integration of the many experiences "out there" into the one unifying principle within each of us. Seen this way, faith is what helps get us on our feet rather than just keeping us on our knees. Spirituality is a state of being in which we finally understand that a miracle is not a moment

when the natural is superseded, but when it is completely ful-
filled. Spirituality is a time when we truly understand that reason is not a luxury we cannot afford, but a necessity without
which we cannot function and without which we certainly
cannot build a global society, the proverbial "city on the hill."
It is a time when we see rational thought and logic as friends
rather than suspected and feared enemies, against which we
must protect ourselves and our children.

But enough with the generalities. Enough with the
exhortations. It is time now to ask and answer the question
that stands before us as a daring challenge: What, then, is this
well-reasoned faith in which I have been urging you to place
your trust? What are its components?

A WELL-REASONED FAITH

Chutzpah is the Yiddish word for nerve. It is a word that is now
part of the lexicon of most people who live in or around major
population centers, especially on the two coasts. I bet even
most people who live in Cleveland or Chicago or Houston
have heard or used the word.

It takes real chutzpah for anyone to try to outline for
another the components of a well-reasoned faith. Faith is such
a personal matter that what one person says can, at best, only
partially satisfy (or dissatisfy) another. But since I have gone
this far, and being near the end of this imaginary literary dock,
I might just as well take the plunge. I have nowhere to go but
in. If some of what follows resonates with you, fine. If not,
then fashion a faith that better fits your needs. Only one thing
I ask: be honest with yourself and try to avoid the easy bro-
midic answers.

SELF

Any faith worthy of a personal commitment needs to begin with a belief in oneself. One of the first Hebrew songs we teach our students in religious school is a catchy little tune with words attributed to Hillel, a great first-century Judaic scholar: "If I am not for myself, who will be for me? If I am only for myself, what am I? And if not now, when?" This aphorism comes very close to saying it all. Until and unless one has a healthy ego, one will not only be unable to lead or guide others, but one will also find oneself unable to make up one's own mind and thus become easy prey for others who have strong opinions and even stronger convictions. A sense of self and confidence in one's own critical capacities are the basis for all independence, all freedom, all judgment, all meaning.

Viktor Frankel was a distinguished Austrian psychiatrist who survived three years in Hitler's concentration camps, including Auschwitz. After the war, his camp experiences led him to found logotherapy, a psychiatric approach that, in his words, "makes the concept of man into a whole . . . and focuses its attention upon mankind's groping for a higher meaning in life." His remarkable book *Man's Search for Meaning* describes not only his camp experiences but also how and why, under identical conditions of camp life, some people survived and others gave up and died. The answer lay in the way each individual thought of himself or herself. "Psychological observations of the prisoners have shown that only the men who allowed their inner hold on their moral and spiritual selves to subside eventually fell victim to the camp's degenerating influences," Frankel wrote. As long as they found some meaning in their day-to-day existence, as long as they looked forward to some small survival goal, they had a better chance of making it than those who lived only in the past. "Any attempt at fighting the camp's psychopathological influence on the prisoner . . . had to aim at giving him inner strength by pointing out to him a future goal to which he could look forward," Frankel continued. A prisoner who lost faith in his or her future was doomed. This faith was pinioned on a sense of self-worth: "I am worthwhile. I have something to live for." Frankel lived by a quotation from the philosopher Friedrich Nietzsche: "He who has a *why* to live for can bear with almost any *how*." He explained, "Woe to him who saw no more sense in his life, no aim, no purpose, and therefore no point in carrying on."

The eminent psychiatrist Erich Fromm made the same point in his writings. In *Man for Himself* he wrote, "My own self, in principle, must be as much an object of my love as another person. The affirmation of one's own life, happiness, growth, freedom, is rooted in one's capacity to love. If an individual is able to love productively, he loves himself too; if he can love only others, he cannot love at all." It is of more than passing interest that early-first-century rabbis interpreted the famous biblical phrase "Thou shalt love thy neighbor as thyself" to mean "You shall love your neighbor, he is yourself." A faith in which one can place reliance begins with the security of believing first in oneself and one's own capacities.

THE POLITICS OF GOD

"If I am only for myself, what am I?" A well-reasoned faith is independently formed but not solipsistic. It does not isolate a person from humanity; it does not allow an individual to turn away from the needs of others. A well-reasoned faith does not pretend that all human beings are good or kind or honest. That naive, idealistic notion of humanity, if it ever really existed, died in the post–World War II era. We know with a certainty born of every human being's experience that there are some right and proper "no-goodniks" walking around out there, against whom we need to protect ourselves and society. We also know that there are millions of people who, through no fault of their own, need our help. Injustice abounds in the world. The rabbis of the Talmudic period tell us that "the sword comes into the world because of justice delayed or justice denied." A well-reasoned faith has a strong social justice component at the core of its theology challenging its adherents. In Judaism, we call this the prophetic imperative. In Christianity, it is known as the social gospel. Its goal: the repair of a broken world. In Hebrew the phrase is *tikkun olam.*

This demand to right society's ills has its origins in the messages of the literary prophets — Amos, Hosea, Isaiah, Jeremiah, and others. It was they who cried out against the injustice of their day: "Woe unto you who join house to house, who add field to field, until there is no more room and you are made to dwell alone in the land" (Isa. 5:8); "Cease to do evil and learn to do right. Pursue justice and champion the oppressed; give the orphan his rights, plead the widow's cause" (Isa. 1:17). Religion has always been involved in what has been called the "politics of God." This has not always made all of its constituents happy. In fact, religion's involvement in the affairs of society has often caused divisiveness within the church community and brought as much misery to society as relief. Nevertheless, as Erich Fromm wrote in *You Shall Be As Gods,* "It must be added that God acts in history and reveals himself in history. This idea has two consequences:

one, that belief in God implies a concern with history and, using the word in its widest sense, a *political* concern. 'Political' here means that they are concerned with historical events affecting not only Israel but all the nations of the world."

In Judaism, the politics of God is as old as the Bible. The literary prophets brought the demand for justice and equity to a high art beginning in the seventh century B.C.E. But 250 years earlier, the prophet Nathan confronted King David to demand a moral accounting. David had arranged for the death of Bathsheba's husband in battle so that he could obtain her as his wife. We can only imagine Nathan's righteous outrage as he, risking his life, stood before his monarch to rebuke him: "David, thou art the man. . . . Why have you despised the word of the Lord, to do what is evil in his sight? You have smitten Uriah the Hittite with the sword, and have taken his wife to be your wife" (2 Sam. 12:1–9). What you have done is reprehensible, and you will be punished for your action. He was. David and Bathsheba's first child died in infancy.

The politics of God, as unfashionable as it has always been, has never gone out of fashion. The remembered giants of religion — men such as Martin Luther, Sir Thomas More, Walter Rauschenbusch, John Haynes Holmes, Rabbi Stephen Wise, and Martin Luther King Jr. — are remembered and admired precisely because of their willingness to speak their religious truth to those in political power so as to effect social change. They made a virtue out of seeking to implement for society the ethical demands of the prophets of Israel.

These men shared one common commitment: they preached and worked for a finer public morality without advocating some specific religion for all. Herein lies the world of difference between them and many of our more contemporary evangelists. Those clergy who pursued the elimination of social evil used the logic of their faith to influence, not to coerce or convert. While motivated by their theologies, they never linked their efforts to a particular brand of organized religion. Nor did they wish to destroy or even erode the wall of separation between church and state. They knew all too well the danger of a faith carried on the sword of a political ruler. Historically, those who disagreed with whoever held that sword died under its blade. A reasoned faith needs emphatically to recommit itself to the pursuit of justice and peace — elusive qualities in contemporary society.

So far, I have outlined values and efforts that any secular humanist can commit to, and to which most do. What distinguishes the religionist from them? God — the belief in and commitment to a God understood as the source of all caring and the model for all human response.

GOD

The final and most demanding component of a well-reasoned faith asks of its adherents that they show respect for Divinity, listen for God's voice in the world, and respond when they think they hear it. It is there. It is the still, small voice of conscience. It is our response to the voices of those who cry out, "Help me." In his book *The Shaking of the Foundations*, the distinguished Protestant theologian Paul Tillich called it the Ultimate Ground of Being:

> The name of this infinite and inexhaustible depth and ground of all being is *God*. That depth is what the word *God* means. And if that word has not much meaning for you, translate it, and speak of the depths of your life, of

the source of your being, of your ultimate concern, of what you take seriously without any reservation. Perhaps, in order to do so, you must forget everything traditional that you have learned about God, perhaps even that word itself. For if you know that God means depth, you know much about him.

Such a "definition" of God destroys our images of a God "up there" or "out there." God, in this category of understanding, is the power we invoke from within ourselves to confront what Albert Camus described as "the benign indifference of the universe." It is what draws from us, when we are at our best, the realization that although Camus's description of the universe may be correct, it cannot describe us. If we want to pass it on to our children and grandchildren, we cannot be benignly indifferent to our world and to what goes on in it. God is the name we give to that internal voice that will not leave us alone, that we have to answer to when there is no one else around to see what we do or do not do. Is this real? For most of us it is undeniably present. But for some this inner voice has been so smothered by negative experience that it is unheard and thus inoperative, buried under a mound of abuse and subsequent rationalization. Where that has happened, people are usually embittered, and sometimes their judgment is distorted. They are often a danger to themselves and to others.

Who is this God to which I am drawn? What is this God? Revisit with me the biblical story of Moses in the wilderness of Sinai as God commissioned him to return to Egypt and lead the Israelites out of their bondage (Exodus, chapter 3). Moses was anything but overjoyed by the encounter at the burning bush. He simply did not want the assignment. Besides, he said, even if I go as your emissary, who will I say sent me? From where will I draw my authority? How will I describe you to anyone in a way that will appear halfway credible? In what has to be one of the Bible's most difficult, most enigmatic, most chewed-over passages, God responds: "Ehyeh-Asher-Ehyeh. . . . Thus shall you say to the Israelites. Tell them 'Ehyeh sent me to you.'. . . This shall be my name forever. This my appellation for all eternity" (Exo. 3:14). We can almost hear Moses' response: "Right! Sure! Clear enough! That ought to do it! Go explain *that* to the Egyptians. Go explain *that* to my own people in Goshen. Thanks, but no thanks." And yet, when one thinks about it, it is the only definition that really works. How better to define the undefinable?

The Hebrew word *Ehyeh* is the first person singular of the verb "to be" (*hayah*). It is the root of one of the Bible's names for God, Yahovah, which when the Bible was translated into Latin became Jehovah. In this first person singular tense, the word could mean "I am" or "I will be." Most biblical commentators take "Ehyeh-Asher-Ehyeh" to convey the future tense: "I will be what I will be." This is taken to mean that I, God, will be understood as I will be understood by every future generation. I, God, may in actuality be a constancy, but I can see how each generation will understand me in its own terms. I can live with that.

We do not know whether or not Moses understood God's response as the commentators interpreted it, but he seemed sufficiently satisfied to go back to Egypt with it. Besides, the bush, burning as it was at the moment without burning up, probably also left him scratching his head in a combination of wonder and confusion. He must have buried this futuristic, fluid definition pretty deep within himself, for there is not a single instance in the Bible where he is shown to have actually used this description. The Midrash (an early-second-century allegorical interpretation of Bible texts) tells us, "while God is called by many names, He is what He is by virtue of His deeds. That is to say, you cannot really know Him until you experience Him in your own life" (Plaut Commentary on the Torah).

The critical phrase is "until you experience Him in your own life." How does one do that? How can any of us experience God in our lives? Through prayer? Meditation? Study? Observing nature? Perhaps all of these ways. But they are not what the Midrash suggests. The Midrash here is quite brilliant and a bit tricky, for as you read it, it seems to turn on its head the traditional imagery of God's relationship to us. It suggests, quite correctly I think, that the phrase "His deeds" really means *our* deeds. How do we experience God in our daily lives? By deeds. By doing. By expressing the positive ethical values we associate with Divinity. I call them "oughts." They are the good things we know we ought to be doing every day to satisfy the demand for constructive human interaction we have learned through experience or wisdom, or divine command. They are the social and personal demands that we know we ought to be fulfilling in and with our lives.

God is the word we use to sum up our expression of these values in the world. When we see these activities in operation, we say that God is present, that God has exercised influence and power. The massive voluntary outpouring of human help to New York City immediately after the September 11, 2001, destruction of the twin towers is a classic example of these "oughts" in operation. Such actions reflect the choices we have made and do make every day. They stand as witness to our successes or failures, not God's. Our actions testify to whether or not we experience Divinity in our lives.

Defining God has always been a problem for theologians, philosophers, all of us. In the twelfth century, Judaism's leading philosopher, Moses Maimonides, also struggled with this dilemma. His solution was not only unique for its day; it also permanently shaped Jewish thinking. God, he wrote, can be defined only negatively. We cannot describe God's essence by means of positive attributes, only negative ones, by what God is not. For example, if we say, as we do, that God is one, what we are saying is that God is neither none nor more than one. If we say that God is incorporeal, we are saying that God is without body and cannot be represented in bodily fashion; we are saying that God is completely spirit or force. If we say that God is not impotent, we imply God's omnipotence. If we deny God's ignorance, we affirm by inference that God is knowledgeable. If we say God is not weak, we similarly affirm God's power. God is the unthinkable, the unknowable, the hidden, the silent. When one thinks about all this for a moment, one begins to understand that to say that God "is" is only to say that God acts. And as we know, the Bible, like all descriptions of God in religious literature, is filled with descriptions of God's activity.

Maimonides' contribution to Jewish thought on the subject of God was significant and major. It helped those who believed in God avoid the pitfall of ascribing to God essential characteristics that, if accepted, would inevitably create a logical conflict. How, for example, could we portray God as being simultaneously merciful and just? That is a contradiction in terms. Maimonides' negative theology avoided that pitfall. Without our trying to ascribe these positive attributes to God, God could be understood as the ideal from which humans draw the concept of complete or perfect mercy and justice. Humans might express both, perhaps even at the same time. The summation of all the preceding is really not too difficult to express. God is revealed *through* humanity, not to humanity. That realization places on us the enormous responsibility of every day having to make a place for God in God's world. "Where is God?" asked the prisoner in Auschwitz as he watched a young boy hanging from a scaffold in the camp's parade ground. The answer is still, as it has always been and forever will be, "Wherever *we* let God in." When we deny God entrance into our lives, the emergence of another Auschwitz is always possible.

DESIGN: CRITICAL FOR THE GARDEN AND FOR LIFE

In building a garden, one tries to marry the nature of the plant material with the canons of balance, design, and good taste. Rational thought and logic, together with imagination and a good "eye" on the part of the landscape designer, play important roles in the layout and development of any garden. One ought to design one's life the same way. We need to fuse the disciplines of critical thinking and the results of historical knowledge and scientific truth with our desire to believe in and relate to that which is a part of us yet apart from us. This is a constantly creative process, one in which we endlessly ask ourselves, How did it all happen? Does it have any meaning for us? Can we play a role in the shaping of our world's destiny? Toward what should we strive for our children and grandchildren? Are we on the right track? Many of us feel that finding adequate responses to these questions requires a leap of faith. This religious gardener would not disparage that need. But I would argue that we ought to reduce, as much as we can, the distance of that leap lest we fall into the pitfall of a too easy, too simple belief.

Over the years, people have frequently asked me how I could be a rabbi. I don't seem to either think or talk as a rabbi "should." My beliefs seem too different from those associated with traditional clergy. People seem to expect religionists to "believe" in spite of what they know rather than because of what they know. I understand their bewilderment. Few, if any, ministers, priests, rabbis, or imams have told people to start their journey toward the star called faith with doubt, disbelief, and skepticism. Few have told them that faith comes last, not first, in the struggle to believe.

There is a tough-mindedness that we in the business of religion ought to demand of ourselves and expect from others. This, I acknowledge, is not a popular approach, but there are values more important than popularity. Popularity is something adolescents usually need and seek. I am no longer an adolescent and do not share their cravings or their values. I have lived long enough to know the ephemeral nature of popularity. I see what it has allowed to pass for culture in our society. Refusing to worry about popularity has allowed me the joy of a religious life rich in controversy and excitement. I would not trade one second of that for some comfortable congregation. It is controversy and struggle, inner and outer, that has made being a rabbi such a great and rewarding career. Perhaps that is why I am so attracted to gardening. It is a constant struggle — first external, then from within. It is exciting and ultimately, with great luck, enormously rewarding. Above everything else, a garden is something of value — perhaps not permanent, but of value nonetheless — that one can leave behind as a legacy for all who come after. That thought brings me much joy.